D0072090

Truman
and
Pendergast

Robert H. Ferrell

Truman and Pendergast

University of Missouri Press
Columbia and London

Copyright © 1999 by
The Curators of the University of Missouri
University of Missouri Press, Columbia, Missouri 65201
Printed and bound in the United States of America
All rights reserved
5 4 3 2 1   03 02 01 00 99

Library of Congress Cataloging-in-Publication Data

Ferrell, Robert H.
    Truman and Pendergast / Robert H. Ferrell.
      p. cm.
    Includes bibliographical references and index.
    ISBN 0-8262-1225-5 (alk. paper)
    1. Truman, Harry S., 1884–1972—Friends and associates.
    2. Pendergast, Tom, 1870–1945.   Kansas City (Mo.)—Politics and
government—20th century.   I. Title.
    E814.F483   1999
    973.918'092—dc21   99-12736
                                                          CIP

∞This paper meets the requirements of the
American National Standard for Permanence of Paper
for Printed Library Materials, Z39.48, 1984.

Text design: Stephanie Foley
Jacket design: Susan Ferber
Typesetter: Bookcomp, Inc.
Printer and binder: Edwards Brothers, Inc.
Typefaces: Palatino and Times

For Elizabeth Safly

Contents

Acknowledgments

My thanks to the following individuals who helped in so many ways: Thomas F. Eagleton, Alice Gorman, Jeffrey C. Graf, Louis C. Gualdoni, Sr., Sam Hamra, Jr., William P. Hannegan, Mrs. Roy W. Harper, Ken Hechler, John K. Hulston, Crosby Kemper III, Sara and Gene McKibben, Lana Stein, Mickey McTague, Kenneth Winn. And to the staff of the Harry S. Truman Library in Independence, Missouri: Dennis E. Bilger, Carol Briley, Ray Geselbracht, Elizabeth Safly, Randy Sowell, Pauline Testerman. Similarly, the Franklin D. Roosevelt Library in Hyde Park, New York: Lynn Bassanese, Robert Parks, Mark Renovitch, Nancy Snedeker, Raymond Teichman, Alycia Vivona. John Lukacs, the historian, as always, offered excellent advice. Likewise, the associate directors of the Western Historical Manuscript Collection of the State Historical Society of Missouri, Ann Morris in St. Louis and David Boutros in Kansas City, together with David F. Moore of the search room in Columbia. Beverly Jarrett, director and editor-in-chief of the University of Missouri Press, watched over everything, as did Jane Lago, managing editor. John Brenner edited the result with care and imagination. Lila and Carolyn always help.

Truman
and
Pendergast

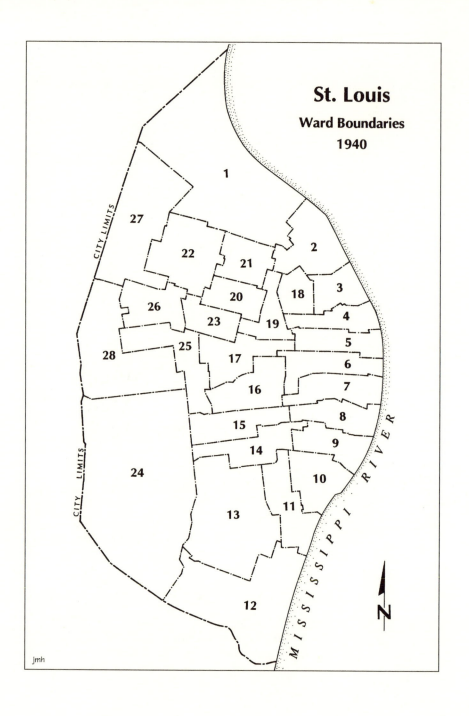

St. Louis

Ward Boundaries

1940

1

27

2

22

21

18

3

20

26

4

23

19

5

28

25

17

6

16

7

8

15

9

14

24

10

11

13

12

MISSISSIPPI RIVER

CITY LIMITS

CITY LIMITS

N

jmh

Ward Vote, City of St. Louis, Democratic Senatorial Primary, August 6, 1940. Office of Secretary of State, Elections Division, Election Returns, Record Group No. 5, Missouri State Archives, Jefferson City.

Ward	Truman	Stark	Milligan
1	3,587	1,738	536
2	1,292	3,173	623
3	711	3,657	227
4	289	2,787	66
5	336	1,900	107
6	2,334	397	174
7	1,076	3,488	296
8	4,022	1,295	557
9	2,723	1,061	378
10	1,703	2,319	737
11	1,852	1,715	514
12	2,299	1,121	314
13	3,358	4,435	1,423
14	1,265	2,317	518
15	1,890	1,917	691
16	2,281	963	313
17	2,052	1,058	378
18	3,487	1,008	357
19	2,538	968	613
20	3,413	953	401
21	2,856	1,079	362
22	4,116	2,697	1,585
23	1,815	1,519	1,060
24	7,831	4,353	1,277
25	1,964	2,811	577
26	2,340	2,791	1,006
27	4,845	4,708	1,709
28	1,877	3,513	945
Totals	70,152	61,741	17,744

Totals for slated candidates in italics; slating as reported by the *St. Louis Post-Dispatch* on election day.

The leading Republican candidate, Manvel H. Davis, received 35,993 votes; the runner-up was David M. Proctor with 18,995. Other candidates were Harold H. Milligan, 7,190; Paul O. Peters, 4,202; William E. Byers, 3,433; Ewing Y. Mitchell, 2,108; H. G. Crosby, 1,863. The total Republican primary vote for senatorial candidates was 73,784; for Democratic candidates, 149,637. The total vote, both parties, was 223,421. Registration was 386,497.

Introduction

Harry S. Truman, one surely must say, enjoyed an honorable relationship with the Democratic boss of Kansas City, Thomas J. Pendergast, during the years when he was a county official in Missouri, down to the time in 1939 when as a U.S. senator he saw the boss sent to Leavenworth for income tax evasion. In Jackson County and in faraway Washington he cooperated on patronage issues with Boss Tom, but did not involve himself in the illegalities and especially the financial dealings that put Pendergast in prison and destroyed the Kansas City machine. Indeed he did not know about most of them.

But being honest did not save him from near defeat during the Missouri senatorial primary in August 1940, when he faced a challenge from Missouri's ambitious governor, Lloyd C. Stark, proprietor of the largest nursery in the United States, the nursery that produced "Stark Delicious" apples. The governor had come into office in 1937, and because the state's constitution limited him to a single four-year term he wanted Truman's Senate seat and set out to get it. In the process he became the destroyer of the Pendergast machine; it was necessary to pull down Truman's sponsor in order to pull down the senator. Stark carefully affixed the stigma of Pendergast upon Truman, even after the boss was in prison.

It is a tangled story, Truman and Pendergast. In its first phase it involved an arm's-length relationship that Truman's later political opponents chose to ignore. The subtleties of Jackson County politics, the distinction in government between the county, which Truman ran, and the city wherein Pendergast conducted political and other business, did not fit the point they wished to make. In Truman's first Senate term he was loyal to the machine, as he had reason to be, but Pendergast did not ask him for favors he should not have granted. Patronage, yes, but that was the stuff of politics in those years of bosses and machines and loyalty. When Truman voted on Senate issues he voted his own judgment, not that of Boss Tom. In the second portion of the relationship, a portion invented by Stark, who denounced Truman as "the Pendergast senator," the factors involved were much different. Truman could say afterward, with a grin, that by defeating Stark he sent the governor back to the nursery. But the 1940 primary fight for renomination to the Senate was no joking matter. In the course of it he came to hate Stark more than any political opponent he ever encountered. And behind Stark was the president of the United States, Franklin D. Roosevelt, whom the governor turned against the senator. Truman had voted a nearly straight New Deal line, but loyalty did not matter when the president needed Missouri's electoral votes in his campaign for a third term and came to believe that Stark could give them to him.

Years have passed, and much new material on Truman and Pendergast has become available. Oral histories came in with tape recorders after World War II and have proved one of the principal resorts for students of American history whose subjects have lived in the recording era. The Harry S. Truman Library in Independence has collected the papers of the president of 1945–1953, which are extraordinarily rich, more informative than those of any other chief executive of the nation, from President George Washington to the present day. Papers of Truman's assistants and friends are in the library. Pendergast kept no papers, but recipients of his letters kept them, and much was written about him in newspapers, and a recent book has gathered this material.[1] Governor Stark died in 1972, the same year as Truman, and the twelve thousand folders containing his papers are in the Western Historical Manuscript Collection of the State Historical Society of Missouri at Columbia. Scattered around the country are the papers of such leading figures as James A. Farley and, in the Franklin D. Roosevelt Library at Hyde Park, New York, those of the Hudson River president who, when he was aiding and abetting Lloyd Stark, never in his most expansive moment thought he was scheming against a future Missouri River president.

The materials for a drawing of relations between Truman and Pendergast are at hand, and the time is right for putting them together, in the era of an Arkansas president.

1

Jackson County to Washington

The two of them, Harry S. Truman and Thomas J. Pendergast, conferred in 1927 over a little issue of four hundred thousand dollars, a road contract that Truman as presiding judge of Jackson County gave to a construction company in South Dakota. Boss Tom, the boss of Kansas City, was none too happy about it. Truman had stood up to the boss and a group of his contractor friends. The boss let the incident pass, and the judge, the principal administrator of the county, was glad for that.

They were fundamentally opposites. Truman was a country man, Pendergast a city man. Truman sometimes was emotional, Pendergast never so. Before he graduated from high school Truman copied off lines from Tennyson's *Locksley Hall*, and carried them in his billfold, copied over many times:

> For I dipt into the future, far as human eye could see,
> Saw the Vision of the world, and all the wonder that
> would be . . .

Pendergast carried no poetry, and by 1927 was skimming money from gambling places and making money from his business enterprises, such as the Ready Mixed Concrete Company. At that time his liquor distributing company was in limbo because of the Eighteenth Amendment but would reemerge when happy times were here again.

Their single common interest was politics. Truman decided to make politics his life's work when he first ran for the county court in 1922. At the outset he was none too good at it, but when he became presiding judge he mastered its requirements. Pendergast was already a master. But he allowed his shrewdness to take him into illegality and would lose all proportion in the mid-1930s, making himself and his machine vulnerable to the enemy who brought him down.

They went different ways, the one becoming president of the United States, the other going to the prison hospital at Leavenworth where he spent a year and a day. A court order confined Pendergast to Kansas City for the remaining few years of his life. He died in 1945 shortly before Truman became president.

1

Truman entered Pendergast's horizons in 1921 when the boss needed a candidate for eastern judge on the court, for the rural part of the county that centered on the farm town of Independence. The court was a three-man body with an eastern judge, a western judge representing Kansas City, and a presiding judge elected at large.

Physically, Harry Truman was no impressive figure to place before voters—he did not cut a figure of a sort that would have made them remember him at the polls. Five-feet-eight and stocky as befitted his rural origins, he was thin-faced, almost sharp-faced, as compared with his appearance in later years. His eyes were warm and friendly, peering from behind the thick-lensed glasses he had worn ever since as a child he was "fine-printed." He possessed a shock of brown hair that was beginning to gray; he was nearly forty years old, having been born in 1884. His appearance was nondescript, and would have allowed him to walk across the square to the Independence courthouse without any resident or stranger so much as glancing at him.

But there were attractions to this man, and they caught Pendergast's attention. They fitted the boss's needs exactly. Truman's family roots reached back nearly to the founding of the state. His forebears had come into Missouri in the 1840s, with a wave of settlers from Kentucky and Illinois. The Trumans came from Kentucky, and so did his relatives on his mother's side, the Youngs. Harry Truman was a Protestant—a Baptist—in a sea of rural Protestants; the Pendergasts in Kansas City were Catholic Irish, and eastern Jackson County was no place for popery. He was a Mason. Joining the order in 1909, he organized a lodge in Grandview, near which village he then was living. His belief in the principles of Masonry lasted through his long life, and was no political affiliation. He was elected to the grand lodge line in 1930.

He had served in the U.S. Army in 1917–1919 and before that in the reserves for six years. War service was important after World War I, and much more so than after World War II when it did not harm the chances of a candidate. In World War I units were raised locally, whereas in World War II, after young men of some localities were raised in units and went to such places as the Philippines and were captured by the Japanese, the practice was abandoned. In 1922 the 129th Field Artillery Regiment, and all the Missouri members of the 35th Division to which the regiment had been attached, stood ready to help with any electoral contest.

His interest in politics had already become evident. In 1914 the then farmer had taken on the petty job of road overseer, upon the death of his father, who had been overseer for his township. Job holding of any sort, if one were a county Democrat, involved a show of party loyalty, and each week he could be seen in the Tenth Ward Democratic Club, which was presided over by Michael J. Pendergast, brother of the Kansas City boss. Truman was not a well-known figure in the club, but years later his by then close friend Tom L. Evans, owner of a chain of Kansas City drugstores, remembered seeing him there.

During the war, and especially after the end of hostilities, when Captain Truman blamed the slowness of the return of Battery D to the United States on officers of the regular army, who desired to keep "the boys" under their command, as well as on the international projects of President Woodrow Wilson (whom he described in letters as "Woodie"), the future president began to talk about taking part in politics. In letters to his fiancée, Bess Wallace, who lived in Independence, he alternated between describing his future occupation as following a mule between two corn rows and seeking election to Congress where he could humble the regular army and its commander-in-chief.

Establishment of the haberdashery delayed his entrance into politics for two or three years. This ill-fated venture begun in 1919 with his army friend Edward Jacobson flourished for a while and then, inadequately financed, collapsed in the recession of 1921–1922. In the summer of 1921 two Pendergasts, Mike and Mike's son Jim, called upon him at the store and pressed the issue early the next year. Truman had known Lieutenant James M. Pendergast in the artillery regiment, although Jim was in another battery. He did a favor for him at one point when Jim was in trouble. In 1921 he and Jim roomed together at the Hotel Robidoux in St. Joseph during the American Legion annual state convention. Early in 1922 the time was right to enter politics; the haberdashery was failing. He had married Bess in 1919 and she hated the idea of moving to the farm, which was what he faced. She would like the notion of his serving as eastern judge, what with the courthouse three blocks from the house in Independence.

In the primary election of 1922 in Jackson County, more important than the November election, Truman received a plurality in a field of six candidates. The Pendergasts were careful to bring in their support after Truman received approval of his veteran friends and the approbation of Colonel William M. Southern, Jr., editor of the *Independence Examiner* and author of a widely read weekly Sunday school lesson. Colonel Southern was the father of one of Truman's sisters-in-law.

Harry Truman served as eastern judge in 1923–1924, failed in his reelection bid because of a division within the Democratic party in the latter year when a Pendergast rival, Joseph B. Shannon, sided with the Republicans, and then received election to two four-year terms as presiding judge, 1927–1930 and 1931–1934.

As presiding judge he achieved a remarkable prominence. During his terms he recognized the need for good roads because of the veritable revolution in production of automobiles in Detroit and elsewhere. At the end of World War I the roads of Jackson County, like those all over the United States, were in terrible condition, hardly fit for buggies and farm wagons, not to mention automobiles and the increasing numbers of trucks. One of Truman's predecessors as presiding judge, Miles J. Bulger, a Kansas City politician known as the "little tsar" because of his stature and tendency to strut, left the county with pie crusts, likely to break with any use and endowed with such design that without any use the water from the slightest cloudburst washed them away. Judge Truman undertook to remedy the road system, barely describable as a system, and employed a nonpartisan panel of two engineers, one Democratic, the other Republican. He went to the county's voters for two bond issues, one for $6.5 million, the other to finish the road program with $3.5 million, and after a campaign of education the issues both passed. When the judge left office he could say with pride that the three-hundred-mile grid of quality cement roads, which brought every farmer in the county to within two miles of a paved road, was one of the finest systems in the country, on a par with Wayne County, Michigan, the county of Detroit, and Westchester County next to New York City. Under his bond issues there was construction of a twenty-two-story art-deco courthouse in Kansas City, replacing a Victorian firetrap, and a refashioning of the courthouse in Independence into a reproduction of Independence Hall in Philadelphia.

The presiding judge managed his construction program, roads and courthouses, with almost no resort to graft. After the first bond issue he gave the large contract to the American Road Building Company of South Dakota, and the result was the meeting with Pendergast in the boss's office. He liked to relate that there he encountered three "Bulger crooks," former friends of the little tsar, by then friends of Pendergast. The judge told the group he had to give contracts to the lowest bidder. Pendergast pressed the issue but Truman was firm. Tom Evans happened to be sitting outside the boss's office and Pendergast had the door open. Tom heard the boss's decision, addressed to the crooked contractors: "I told you he was the hardheadest, orneriest man in the world; there isn't anything I can do. That's it, gentlemen. You get your price right and get the best material. You heard him say it; you'll get the business."[1]

But to set out the judge's qualities and successes is to present only one side of the story, and to make Truman's political progress seem too easy. The other side involved his relations with Pendergast, which were more complicated than the encounter with the crooked road contractors.[2]

Pendergast, like Truman, was unimpressive in appearance. In his youth he possessed the build of a fighter, with big hands, bulging muscles, thick neck, strong face; he sported a Bismarck mustache, and his head was topped with hair. Years of good living, and in the case of the mustache changing fashions, removed most of that. Into his fifties, smooth-shaven, nearly bald, he would have been unrecognizable to his friends of the 1890s. A little taller than Truman at five-feet-nine, he weighed much more, 245 pounds. He still was capable of chastising opponents. When the vice president of an electric light and power corporation came to see him and had the impudence to offer him twenty thousand dollars to advance some sort of legislative measure, "I didn't give him time to explain what it was. I didn't care. I told him 'Get out or I'll break your jaw.' He got out—running." Another visitor sought to misbehave and was knocked through a glass door. The boss offered these details to a reporter for the *St. Louis Post-Dispatch* who placed them in his newspaper.[3]

In dealing with visitors to his office at 1908 Main Street, on the second floor of a brick building that housed the Jackson Democratic Club, he was quick and to the point. He was accustomed to gaze at suppliants with his small, sharp eyes. Questions were short, and upon measuring a situation he dispatched it, for he had no time to waste. If necessary he gave visitors letters to public officials, signed with varicolored ink or pencil. Rumor had it that one color meant "Do what I say" and another meant "Forget it."

In remarking the way that Pendergast appeared to people who saw him in his office and to reporters who ventured into his presence, it is necessary to relate that like most if not all of the bosses of his time and earlier, he had developed an extraordinary political sensitivity. Political bosses have largely passed from the scene, and it is difficult to comprehend what they once were. The cartoonist for the *Post-Dispatch*, Daniel R. Fitzpatrick, was accustomed to drawing Pendergast as a "thick-skulled, heavy-jowled oaf," to use the description of one of the boss's enemies, and it was entirely wrong. The boss was no fool, by any means, and on all political questions he was deft to the point of genius: he could sense an issue before it appeared, and make just the right answer to it if it had the temerity to appear. His ability to balance or undermine opponents was remarkable. He was not accustomed to plan things; he was no philosopher. He took advantage. If observers gave him credit for foresight he took credit, but it was the opportunity that counted. All the while he calculated power, its location, how if he did not control it he could do so.

In a different day and age Pendergast might have been a rich lawyer or banker or businessman. So talented was he that he could have gone in many directions, had opportunity offered. He entered politics because of his older brother James, known as Alderman Jim. When his brother relinquished his duties with Kansas City's first and second wards in 1910, and died of Bright's disease the next year, Tom took over.

It was probably the procedures of his older brother that led him into the temptations, mostly financial, that eventually overwhelmed him. Jim had protected the poor with turkeys for Thanksgiving, chickens for Christmas, coal on all occasions, and had obtained the money by skimming gambling enterprises. When Tom took over he managed the Jefferson Hotel, a third-class hostelry that sponsored a bevy of prostitutes, but soon turned to more respectable sources of income and sold franchises and tax abatements. When the Kansas City streetcar monopoly desired to renew its contract well in advance of the contract's end, to ensure its stranglehold over the city's transportation, Tom was able to handle the problem. At the same time he became an almost too successful businessman. He owned the Ready Mixed Concrete Company. He enlarged his brother's company for distributing liquor, and as his power in Kansas City increased, local saloons found it to their benefit to purchase Pendergast liquor. He was a partner in several other enterprises.

The concrete company, and the W. A. Ross Construction Company of which he was a partner, made him interested in city construction. Among the more controversial projects in which ready-mixed concrete appeared was the paving of Brush Creek, a stream that meandered for fifteen miles through the city. The boss had it paved: it was fifty feet wide and the cement reportedly was a foot and a half thick, although actually it was only eight inches thick. Judge Truman's successful bond issue in 1928 caught Pendergast's attention; he had told the judge it would fail. At the time of Truman's second issue in 1931, Boss Tom sponsored a $29 million issue for the city, which like Truman's county issues was approved by the taxpayers. In addition the city managed federal grants to the amount of $10 million. Counting the county's two bond issues totaling $10 million, the machine spent $50 million in the early years of the Great Depression, a cornucopia of dollars that saved the county and city from the worst of the hard times and helped ensure Pendergast's control.

In his construction projects the boss was assisted by the Kansas City Chamber of Commerce, which was under supervision of Conrad H. Mann, a Republican who first cooperated with Pendergast in arranging the streetcar franchise in 1914. Con Mann was convicted in 1933 of running a lottery that netted him and an associate $460,000, and after his conviction in New York City and removal to the local House of Correction he received a last-minute pardon from President Franklin D. Roosevelt. He returned in triumph to Kansas City, where he received a special welcome arranged by Pendergast, after which he continued his work of assisting the boss with construction under the 1931 bond issue and any other money he and the boss could get their hands on.

Another Pendergast assistant, and a notable one, was City Manager Henry L. McElroy. Truman knew him well, as during his two-year term as eastern judge, 1923–1924, he worked with McElroy, who was western judge. Both lost in the 1924 election, with Truman occupying the next two years selling memberships in the Kansas City Automobile Club and managing an insurance agency and a savings and loan. McElroy became city manager in 1926 when Truman received election as presiding judge.

At the outset McElroy seemed a good city appointee. He had been a member of the real estate firm organized by the developer J. C. Nichols, whose Country Club Plaza to the south of Kansas City's business district, a Moorish extravaganza with a tower, fountains, statuary, and tastefully appointed stores, was one of the first shopping centers in the United States. Behind it lay Nichols's Ward Parkway development of stylish high-priced houses for the city's social and economic elite; in 1931, Pendergast moved his family into a house on the parkway built by Nichols costing $175,000. McElroy himself did not possess Pendergast's financial interests, although while in real estate he laid away half a million dollars, he said, which he claimed proved his honesty because he did not need to take city money. "Listen," he had said when he became western judge on the county court, "I've got $500,000 all my own. I'm going into that court job and give a real business administration." He lived in a modest, square house at 21 West Fifty-seventh Street. Into his sixties when he became city manager, he was notable for his white hair and a face that turned crimson down to his collar when he became angry, which was often. Because of his rages, which he seemed to sponsor for the welfare of the city, he became known as Old Turkey Neck. When not enraged he spoke in pious ways and remarked precepts learned "from my old Presbyterian mother."

But McElroy was utterly subservient to Pendergast, willing to give him any city money he wanted. He defined his connection with Pendergast carefully. "Tom and I are partners," he told a reporter for *American* magazine. "He takes care of politics and I take care of the business of Kansas City. He gives people jobs; I make them work. Every Sunday morning, at Tom's house or at mine, we meet and talk over what's best for the city."[4] The city received notable buildings, including a great new auditorium that occupied an entire block. The parkways instituted by McElroy and watched over in their construction by Con Mann were easily visible and in their ways admirable. But the less said the better about what happened to the money received from the bond issues. Years afterward, upon McElroy's resignation after Pendergast was indicted, investigation of the city's finances revealed $11 million missing from the city manager's accounts, impossible to trace because department heads transferred funds from one account to another, a practice McElroy described, from his rural Iowa origins, as country bookkeeping. How much went to the boss for his own projects, such as trips to Europe aboard transatlantic liners or stays in New York City at the Waldorf-Astoria, was difficult to estimate. After the collapse of the machine it was revealed that the municipal water department repaired water leaks but was not in the business of detecting them, which activity it contracted to the Rathford Engineering Company for $5,000 per month. The Kansas City charter required the city council to approve all contracts exceeding $2,500, but the council never saw the Rathford contract. From 1931 to 1938 the firm received $342,500. Rathford had one full-time employee.[5] After the city's finances were reorganized in 1939–1940, the number of leaks diminished. Meanwhile a great deal of Ready Mixed cement proved necessary for city construction projects. McElroy provided many city jobs. It turned out that not always was there any connection of jobs with work done. After the machine's collapse it became evident that the city carried thousands of employees on its rolls whose sole work consisted of coming in for their checks.

The machine's governance of Kansas City, under the boss's direction, with the assistance of Con Mann and City Manager McElroy, obviously left something to be desired. It was a shoddy management, rife with corruption. The entire city government became a machine within the machine, having as its purpose the furnishing of whatever funds the Pendergast machine needed.

Some of the machine's behavior bordered on the humorous. Unusual services were provided. If tires disappeared from a voter's car, and he reported this loss to the police department, it was possible to have the tires put back on the car during the night. The police would get in touch with "Fat Willie," who had the tire-stealing concession in the city, and inform him that his men had taken tires from the wrong car. Fat Willie would arrange for the tires to be reinstalled, which his concession required. The machine thus did a favor for a voter, and the voter could feel that being a part of the machine provided a kind of free insurance.

Then in 1927 there was a reinterpretation by the Missouri Supreme Court of a 1905 statute banning betting on horses. Pendergast was an inveterate fan of horse racing, and his hand was in the reinterpretation. Through a loophole in the statute, permitted by the reinterpretation, an individual could make a contribution for improvement of a horse's breed. A test was necessary. If the animal whose breeding was being assisted by the contribution happened to run, perhaps minutes later, in competition against other horses, on an oval track with lines at the start and finish, and ran first, the investor in the horse's breed became eligible for a "refund." The racetracks had windows labeled "Contributions" and "Refunds."

Any humor seen in the operations of Boss Tom's machine had to be set against the enormous cost of the boss's lifestyle and of unfulfilled bond issues. Too, Kansas City was a wide-open place in which anything went, with gambling day and night in the city's downtown. Anything was available, and Maurice M. Milligan, who became United States attorney for the western district of Missouri in 1934, remarked in a later book the judgment of the *Omaha World Herald*, which advised, "If you want to see some sin, forget about Paris and go to Kansas City. With the possible exception of such renowned centers as Singapore and Port Said, Kansas City probably has the greatest sin industry in the world."[6]

Gangsters thrived in the city. Federal law officers told Milligan that during the 1930s there was a crime corridor from St. Paul through Chicago with its focal point in Kansas City. One of Pendergast's lieutenants until his demise in a fusillade of machine-gun bullets in 1934, a handsome young man who dressed impeccably, John Lazia, had entered politics under the tutelage of the ward captain of "Little Italy," a Pendergast associate, Michael Ross. After marriage in 1924, Lazia organized a soft-drink distributorship for Golden Mist, a distasteful beverage that his assistants forced upon stores. In 1928 he displaced his mentor Ross, who had moved out of his ward and did not deserve it anyway because he was not Italian. Soon Lazia claimed he could vote seventy-five hundred people. Pendergast recognized him in part because he, the boss, could do nothing else. In 1932 when the Kansas City Police Department passed from state to local control, which the city's reformers hailed as a triumph of local government, Lazia recruited new officers, hiring sixty recently released convicts from Leavenworth for second careers in law enforcement. An estimate had it that 10 percent of police officers possessed criminal records. The next year Lazia helped Charles "Pretty Boy" Floyd obtain an assistant in attempting the release of a fellow gangster under custody, resulting in the so-called Union Station Massacre conducted in broad daylight in the station's parking lot, which killed four law enforcement officers and the prisoner. Lazia assisted the would-be liberators in escaping the city. Because one of the slain lawmen was an FBI agent, who according to custom at that time was unarmed, the bureau asked for and received permission from Congress to arm its agents.

That Kansas City became a sanctuary for the nation's gangsters did not mean the Pendergast machine was safe from criminals. Pendergast's house was robbed of $150,000 in cash and other items. City Manager McElroy's daughter was kidnaped and released upon payment of $30,000 ransom.

In the early 1930s two almost pitiful efforts took place within the city to free it from the machine. The first began when the young rabbi of Temple B'nai Jehudah, Samuel S. Mayerberg, galvanized a group of club women in 1932 by telling them their city had passed out of control into that of the machine's principal figures. He went to the ministerial association and its members cheered his description of what had happened to Kansas City. He and his supporters organized what they described as the Charter League, asking enforcement of the charter by which the city administration had passed to McElroy, controlled by Pendergast.

The leader of the initial reform movement, Rabbi Mayerberg, was a very able man, a large personality. Brought up in the South, a graduate of Hebrew Union College in Cincinnati, he was a masterful speaker; his reviews of newly published books drew fifteen hundred attendees. He would have led the righteous citizens of Kansas City if anyone could have. Eyes flashing, he spoke with the prophet Jeremiah: "And seek the peace of the city, and pray unto the Lord for it; for in the peace thereof shall ye have peace." But he could not keep his movement going, and within months the Charter League was dead. During World War II he returned to Hebrew Union for a series of lectures, later published. Elegant, written with verve, they set out his deeply religious principles and in two chapters his hopes for the city in which he spent most of his life. He was proud, he wrote, to follow the course advised in a poem by a nameless author:

> God, make my life a little light
> Within the world to glow,
> A little flame that burneth bright
> Wherever I may go.[7]

A group of young businessmen led by a paint salesman named Joseph C. Fennelly organized what they described expansively as the National Youth Movement, which they hoped might defeat the machine. In 1934 they put up a slate headed by a former president of the University of Missouri, A. Ross Hill. Like Mayerberg, they went down to defeat, in a city election marked by extraordinary violence, in which gangs of machine goons roamed the streets in automobiles without license plates, while the police stood by. Dozens of youths, many of them college students, were beaten up; there were four deaths, eleven people severely injured, and many bruises, black eyes, and cracked heads. A reporter for the *Kansas City Star*, which had championed the NYM and supported Mayerberg two years before, was chased from street to street until in near terror he managed the safety of the building of his paper.

The truth was that in the early 1930s reform had no champions except Mayerberg and Fennelly and club women and the ministerial association and the *Star* and the NYM's young businessmen and the college students. The city's principal businessmen stood back, as they had made their peace with the machine and enjoyed special franchises and tax abatements. The populace went along because McElroy had so many jobs created by country bookkeeping if not advice from his old Presbyterian mother.

And what was Truman to do about all this? He found himself in a real quandary. He was administratively removed from the city, being administrator of the county, which meant mostly the eastern portion around Independence and a few rural townships south of the city around Grandview. In the county area he possessed a personal authority. When Mike Pendergast died in 1929—Mike had handled eastern county matters from the tenth ward club—Boss Tom made Judge Truman his representative in the eastern part of the county. Years later, after he was president, Truman related the result: "I controlled the Democratic Party in Eastern Jackson County when I was county judge. . . . In any election I could deliver 11,000 votes and not steal a one. It was not necessary. I looked out for people and they understood my leadership."[8] Judge Truman was largely an independent force politically. For county issues it was necessary for Pendergast to negotiate with him. Nonetheless, the arrangement meant some cooperating. Truman was careful to give county jobs to deserving Democrats, which meant Pendergast Democrats, for they could do the work as well as ordinary Democrats, certainly as well as Republicans, of whom there were not all that many in the county.

For Truman, another embarrassment was that Pendergast could count on the presiding judge's reputation for honesty to assist whatever projects the boss had in mind in the city. Pendergast could point with pride to the fact that the city's leading newspaper, the *Kansas City Star*, anti-Pendergast since the 1890s, described Judge Truman as "extraordinarily efficient," said that "not a suspicion of graft has developed," and championed Truman against Republican opponents in the elections of 1926 and 1930.[9]

Still another was that despite the judge's best efforts some of the grafting, not much but a little, spilled over into county business.

Dealing with Pendergast was no easy thing to do, and Truman sought to gather his thoughts on the subject. When unclear about his purposes he was accustomed to sit down quietly somewhere and write out his thoughts. The words, he hoped, would make his thoughts more clear. Early in the 1930s he went to the assistant manager of a hotel in Kansas City, the Pickwick, and asked for a room to which, as a busy official, he might repair for the purpose of quiet and uninterrupted time so he might, to mention one purpose, read books about history. Another was to be by himself, without the telephone or people coming to ask favors or offer unsolicited suggestions on complicated matters. The assistant manager was entirely understanding, and made the arrangement. The result was more reading and some contemplation, and in the latter regard a sheaf of handwritten papers bearing the name of the hotel, which would become known to historians and political scientists as the Pickwick papers when they became available at the Harry S. Truman Library in Independence after the writer of the papers passed on.[10]

The Pickwick papers set out their author's dissatisfaction over the predicament he found himself in. When he was elected presiding judge in 1926 he arranged for a suitable man to be elected eastern judge, so he and his man could control the court against whatever grafter was elected western judge in Kansas City. Robert Barr seemed upright and attractive. A graduate of West Point, he was a gentleman farmer. He took part in the war, and something about the war shattered his health; he died young. But Truman's plan for Barr's role went astray. The West Pointer showed less spine than Truman counted on, and forced the presiding judge into letting "a former saloon keeper and murderer, a friend of the Big Boss, steal about $10,000 . . . from the general revenues of the County." The compromise was necessary "to satisfy my ideal associate and keep the crooks from getting a million or more out of the bond issue."

Truman asked himself, concerning the money that Barr cost the county, "Was I right or did I compound a felony?" He knew, and so wrote in the Pickwick paper, that by dispensing the money, a relatively small sum, he probably saved much more—that by not making an issue of the loss he did not compound his own contention with the boss in front of the crooked road contractors and lose Pendergast's support in the forthcoming election in 1930 for a second four-year term. The boss told him that in Kansas City every bid for a contracting job was doctored so "the inside gentlemen" secured the contract. Pendergast indirectly was telling Truman to go and do likewise. Truman had not gone down the broad way that leadeth to destruction, but there was a price.

In one of the Pickwick papers he wrote of saving $1 million, in another of saving $3.5 million, which apparently meant he was able to handle the second bond issue without interference. It is difficult to know exactly what he was writing about. He may have been calculating what it meant to employ Pendergast Democrats for county work, not other Democrats or Republicans, and purchase supplies from Pendergast companies or the boss's friends and supporters. "I wonder," he wrote, "if I did right to put a lot of no account sons of bitches on the payroll and pay other sons of bitches more money for supplies than they were worth in order to satisfy the political powers and save $3,500,000.00."

The future president wrote that the boss of Kansas City had good and bad traits. He set them out confusingly. "I am obligated to the Big Boss, a man of his word; but he gives it very seldom and usually on a sure thing. But he's not a trimmer. He in times past owned a bawdy house, a saloon and gambling establishment, was raised in that environment but he's all man. I wonder who is worth more in the sight of the Lord?" He remembered machines of the past and the moment, and thought "maybe machines are not so good for the country." He wrote that "Tammany, Bill Thompson, Mr. Cox of Cincinnati, Ed Butler, they all have but one end—fool the taxpayer, steal the taxes. The 'people' are dumb." He thought that "there are 'machines' and machines." He did not know what he and every other resident of Jackson County discovered a few years later when Pendergast got into trouble, that the Kansas City machine was not better than the others. He underestimated crookedness in the Kansas City of Pendergast, McElroy, and Lazia. The metropolis, he avowed, had "an extraordinarily clean" government: "Chicago, Pittsburgh, San Francisco, Los Angeles make us look like suckers."

2

Truman went to the Senate in 1935, having received Pendergast's support during the statewide election of the preceding year, and it was at this time that he began to be known to his detractors as "the gentleman from Pendergast." The origin of the phrase is unclear, and it is possible that the boss invented it. According to what people said, Pendergast on one occasion waxed expansively on how he advanced Truman to the national scene. Big business, he explained, had its representatives, and he wanted to send his own man.[11]

Truman was known as Pendergast's office boy. The veteran head of the Missouri Farmers' Association, William Hirth, referred to him as a "bell-hop." A Truman opponent in the campaign of 1934 said that as a senator he would get "calluses on his ears listening on the long-distance telephone to the orders of his boss."

The Senate nomination came at an extraordinary time in Truman's political career, and he was enormously grateful to Pendergast for it. The boss had his own reasons for sponsoring Truman, and the presiding judge understood some of them, but the truth was that in 1934 it was beginning to appear that Truman had come to the end of his political possibilities. The custom in Missouri politics was that after two terms in a county office it was necessary to pass the office to another individual—that two terms were enough. Early that year Truman was almost desperately looking for another place, hoping against hope that something would turn up, altogether unsure of what the boss had in mind, if Pendergast had anything in mind. Moreover, Truman's need to find something to do, presumably a political something to do, was vastly complicated by the Great Depression, which was so much in evidence in Missouri as well as across the entire country. Jobs of any sort, public or private, were so difficult to discover. As in 1922 when the haberdashery was failing, he faced the prospect of going back to the farm, which would have been such an embarrassment for him because Bess so disliked the farm and desired to stay in Independence where she had been born and grew up.

Prior to the nomination he had tried for several offices. Despite the adage of American politics that the office must come to the man, Truman knew that in any real-life situation it was necessary to nudge the office. At the outset he reached as high as he could, seeking the governorship.[12] On September 19, 1929, a small newspaper, the *Clinton Eye*, had begun advocating Truman for governor, this in the election coming up in 1932. The Truman boom for the highest state office did not display progress, and not until more than a year later, on November 14, 1930, did the *Odessa Democrat* come out for Truman. A week later, in the Kansas City suburb of Fairmount, the *Blue Valley*

Inter-City News joined the outcry, quoting the Odessa paper. Early next year Truman's cousin Ralph began a movement to get the judge to Jefferson City; the candidate said he was no candidate but if a situation developed, Missourians "might find me ready at their command to enter the lists."

Suddenly the effort to obtain the governorship collapsed, for Pendergast declared for the unsuccessful Democratic candidate of 1928, Francis M. Wilson, a poetical, oratorical fellow, a great Missouri statesman type, dignified yet humorous, possessed of red hair and freckles and known as the Red Headed Peckerwood of the Platte. He was from Platte City, twenty miles northwest of Kansas City. Judge Truman retired from the fray.

The next possibility was twofold, for Truman helped in a statewide redistricting for congressmen and created a new fourth Missouri district that included Independence and its rural hinterland and a small part of Kansas City, an ideal gerrymander for himself. If that did not work there was the county collectorship, an office with a large income from fees that made up for any lack of dignity. The congressional seat meant residence in Washington for part of each year and dealing with national issues. The collectorship could take him out of debt; the haberdashery was a partnership and he became responsible for all its debts, which by 1929 totaled in principal and accumulated interest $8,944.78, a sum that hung over him like a cloud.

Unfortunately, the dual possibility of a congressional seat and the collectorship came to naught, disappeared over his horizon. The seat went to a circuit judge, formerly a member of the city council, C. Jasper Bell, to whom Pendergast was beholden for constituting a bare majority in the council organized under the amended city charter; Bell gave the city to the boss, and something needed to be done. Truman later wrote, "I wanted to be Congressman from the new fourth Missouri district but a circuit judge wanted it also and the dignity of the court had to be upheld."[13] After Bell went to Congress to become a great expert on the Philippines, a subject suitably removed from issues in Kansas City with which he had been familiar, Truman and Pendergast doubtless smiled when they thought of his translation to the national scene. The collectorship also was under management of Boss Tom, and the boss assigned it to a friend of the Kansas City banker William T. Kemper. As Truman thought about that arrangement he liked to say that Pendergast had been in the pocket of Kemper. The truth was that Kemper and Pendergast both had large pockets and liked to help each other. Kemper had been in Kansas City politics since the turn of the century, and had arranged for Truman to be a page at the Democratic national convention held in Kansas City in 1900. In 1934 he held no malice for Truman, and indeed the next year assisted Truman's brother Vivian in repurchase of the note representing the haberdashery debts; it was a large note, which had passed from one bank to another, and having proved uncollectible because Truman was a public official and could not be sued it finally was discounted and sold at a sheriff's sale for one thousand dollars. Kemper pulled a string or two for Truman to get it. Kemper meanwhile was hand in glove with Pendergast because through the boss the banker might arrange deposit of state funds, often millions of dollars, in Kemper's bank, the Commerce Trust Company. State deposits did not draw interest.

What Truman did not realize early in 1934 when he was attempting almost desperately to find a place for himself was that fortune was pushing him toward the Senate because there he would fit into a larger scheme of things. At the beginning the scheme may not have been in the mind of the boss of Kansas City. But Pendergast was a shrewd man, of long local experience, and as each opportunity presented itself he seized it, constructing nothing less than a triumphal arch for his ambition to be a statewide and even national leader.[14]

There can be no question that when opportunity knocked, Boss Tom was ready. His initial triumph had been the amendment of the Kansas City charter in 1925 that placed the metropolis under a city manager, a then popular arrangement urged nationwide by political scientists. All he had to do was obtain a majority of seats in the city council, appoint the manager, and have everything in his hands. That was where Jasper Bell, the Philippine expert, came in. After that the manager was everything, the mayor nothing. After construction in the 1930s of a new skyscraper city hall, one of McElroy's first acts was to give himself a spacious office on the twenty-ninth floor and consign Mayor Bryce B. Smith to a closet around the corner.

Taking over the city under the aegis of good government, the boss in 1932 found himself the recipient of a gift from a Missouri Republican governor, Henry F. Caulfield, whose training in political science was incomplete. The state lost population and it was necessary to rearrange congressional districts, in which task Judge Truman assisted, constructing his gerrymander. The Democratic legislature created gerrymanders all over the state, ensuring the party's control of eight districts. The governor should have realized that eight small Democratic beasts were tolerable, but did not. He vetoed the rearrangement, and in the congressional elections of 1932 it was necessary for all Missouri congressmen to run at large. This gave Pendergast, with his huge voting machine in the state's western metropolis, a large say in their elections. There were fifty-six candidates; Pendergast slated twenty-two, and most of them won—full of gratitude for his support.

In 1932 the boss's candidate for the governorship, Francis Wilson, seemed a shoo-in. But a surprising development provided a better, indeed much better, inhabitant of the governor's mansion in Jefferson City. Wilson had a statewide following. He might have given Boss Tom trouble if he had been elected, for he was honest and independent. The boss endorsed him because of his prominence and the need to support a winning candidate; he had little choice. But the candidate was getting up in years, sixty-four in 1932, and had recovered from an operation for stomach ulcers. After winning the primary, Wilson came down with another attack of ulcers and died. What to do? Wilson died on October 12, twenty-five days before the November election, and to get the candidate's name printed on the ballot it had to be sent in ten days before the election. Wilson's family and friends asked Pendergast to endorse a fellow resident of Platte City, a circuit judge by the name of Guy B. Park. Pendergast had never heard of him and asked, "Who the hell is Park?" Recovering from surprise, he decided that Park's slating was the proper thing to do in memory of the departed Red Headed Peckerwood. When he discussed the issue at a meeting of the state's politicians in Jefferson City a rebellion threatened; the boss told the assembled leaders who he was for and after a little muttering they quieted down. Park was notified, and according to what Pendergast told a reporter for the *St. Louis Post-Dispatch*, the news came like a thunderbolt. Pendergast's principal lieutenant in Kansas City, the state chairman of the Democratic party, James P. Aylward, took charge of Park, and as Jim long afterward remembered, he "dragged him over the state," fast as he could, and elected him.[15] Park was so grateful for his elevation that during the four years of his term he did anything Boss Tom desired.

Guy Park was a far more pliant occupant of the governor's office than Wilson would have been. The boss told the *Post-Dispatch* reporter laconically that "He was a nice gentleman."[16] Park understood Kansas City politics. During his governorship a young student from Illinois wrote him that she was doing a theme on the Pendergast machine and could he tell her what it was? "The so-called Pendergast machine," the governor responded,

> is an organization of fighting Democrats built up on service and achievement. It has its captains and lieutenants running down to every block in Kansas City. Between elections these workers spend much time and money looking after the welfare of the unfortunate people of the community, caring for them in case of illness or when they are out of work. And naturally, when election day comes, these people are loyal to those who have helped them in time of need.[17]

Once Park was installed, it was said that Pendergast's office on Main Street was the state capitol and the governor's mansion in Jefferson City was Uncle Tom's Cabin.

In 1932, Pendergast led Missouri's delegation to the national convention in Chicago, and it is entirely possible that he again seized an opportunity to increase the power of his machine. According to one story the boss had been troubled by the presidential ambitions of former senator James A. Reed, with whom he and his brother Alderman Jim had been allied ever since Reed was mayor of Kansas City at the turn of the century. Indeed Reed had appointed Tom Pendergast to the street cleaning department. The silver-tongued Reed looked like a Roman and had a large personal following. During his Senate years he cut a swathe in national and even international politics. In 1917 he asked President Wilson to appoint his friend Robert Emmet O'Malley as postmaster of Kansas City (O'Malley will appear later in these pages), and when Wilson refused he turned against him, leading the band of "irreconcilable" senators who in 1919–20 defeated the Treaty of Versailles and prevented the United States from joining the League of Nations. It was possible to contend that America forsook the League and, as some writers put it, "broke the heart of the world," destroying the peace after World War I, because Wilson turned down the moon-faced O'Malley. Reed was seventy-one years old in 1932, and insisted upon being designated

Missouri's favorite son at the Chicago convention. He may have embarrassed Pendergast, who (according to the story) wanted to get on the bandwagon of Governor Roosevelt. But the boss profited from Reed's ambition. A year before the convention, so the story had it, he made a private deal with Roosevelt's backers and when he took his state's delegation to Chicago pledged to Reed he carefully avoided placing its members under a unit rule that would require voting for Reed, allowing them to make their own decisions. This was important to the Roosevelt people, fearful that in successive ballots their candidate's total might begin to move down. Not knowing what Pendergast had arranged, the Missouri delegates behaved exactly as the boss and the Roosevelt people desired. On the first ballot the St. Louis leader Louis Jean Gualdoni took a group of rebels over to Roosevelt. On each ballot thereafter there were defections, until the victorious fourth ballot when the entire delegation voted for FDR. Publicly the boss supported Reed, and when Gualdoni defied him, as the account goes, he threatened a fistfight. After the Chicago theatrics his reward was the state's federal patronage, given as soon as the Roosevelt administration came into office.

The alternative story was not so much to Pendergast's credit and in one particular seems much more likely to have been true. It credits Pendergast with having been sincerely in support of Reed. As for threatening to beat up Jean Gualdoni, the boss never did propose such a course: Gualdoni in his early years had been a professional fighter, and in seventeen matches knocked out fifteen opponents, won another fight by decision, and fought once to a draw.[18]

Regardless of which candidate Pendergast backed in Chicago, the Democrats won the presidency in November and President Roosevelt gave the federal patronage to the Kansas City boss. Perhaps the only problem with the halcyon year 1932 was that Boss Tom failed to elect his nominee for the Senate seat vacated by a Democrat and St. Louisian, Harry B. Hawes. In the primary the boss endorsed a Kansas City corporation lawyer, Charles M. Howell. Bennett Champ Clark, an upstart with a famous name, from Bowling Green, near St. Louis, defeated Pendergast's man. Clark's father, Champ Clark, had been Speaker of the House of Representatives and in 1912 came close to obtaining the Democratic nomination for the presidency, until defeated by a dark horse, Woodrow Wilson. Of average height, pudgy, even porcine, with a pumpkin face, the son possessed many qualities of the father, including quickness. He was a great stump speaker in the Missouri tradition and could skewer an opponent with a phrase or two. He easily did it to Howell, and indelicately campaigned against Pendergast, mentioning the boss by name and skewering him. Pendergast did not admire such tactics, and in 1934, when the state's other Senate seat came up and was vulnerable to Democratic assault, being held by a Republican prohibitionist, Roscoe C. Patterson (named after a forgotten nineteenth-century Republican worthy, Roscoe Conkling), he determined to nominate a winning candidate not merely to represent Kansas City but also to humiliate Clark.

In 1934 the omens for nominating and electing a senator were far better than two years before. Patterson was a sitting duck. Election of Park as governor gave Pendergast leverage. As Aylward remembered,

> By reason of the election of Park, why, Pendergast became a statewide leader. He was in a position to obtain jobs for members of the faithful not only here but all over the state, and thereby build up a statewide organization that would go along with any reasonable program suggested to them; and that's how he became powerful enough to be in a position to offer a candidate for the Senate and had more than a reasonable chance of nominating and electing the candidate to the United States Senate . . .[19]

The question was whom to nominate, and on that score the boss was uncertain. He at first chose his state chairman, Aylward. Jim did not like the idea of a nomination that would involve a fight with rival machine politicians in St. Louis; the St. Louis leaders seldom agreed with anyone in Kansas City. Behind them would be Clark with his sharp tongue. An ethical lawyer with a large Kansas City practice and income, he would lose it if he went to Washington. The boss asked the defeated candidate of 1932, Howell, who anticipated a more difficult fight than before and wanted none of it. He asked Joe Shannon, with whom he had made up and exiled to Congress. Joe looked like President Warren G. Harding, and in Congress took on the role of a Jeffersonian idealist, which was all right, but he also became a Roosevelt hater, which in Missouri politics in the early 1930s was not all right. Shannon may have seen a sly effort to get him defeated, which would lose him his safe congressional district;

he enjoyed sitting around the Mayflower Hotel lobby in Washington and did not want to go back to Kansas City. Apparently former senator Reed was informed of the opening, but Reed was too old and by this time knew it. He also could have had the same impression attributed to Shannon, that Pendergast wanted him to be nominated and lose. Reed, incidentally, had endorsed Clark in 1932, a gross act in the eyes of Pendergast, even though the former senator had nominated Clark's father at the Democratic national convention in 1912 and endorsement of the son should have been understandable.

Choosing a candidate came down to a meeting between Aylward and Pendergast, in which the state chairman put forward the names of ten prominent people in Kansas City and environs.[20]

"I don't know any of them," growled the boss.

"What kind of a senator do you want?" asked Aylward.

"I'd like to have someone I can talk to—close enough to talk to," was the response.

"That's reasonable," agreed Aylward. "Well," he added, "why don't you run Harry S. Truman for the United States Senate? He's a former soldier. He soldiered with Jim here, your nephew [Jim was present]. He's a member of the Masonic Order; he's a Baptist; he's been active in affairs around here."

"Nobody knows him," said the boss. "He's an ordinary county judge and not known outside Jackson County." Then the idea took hold. "Do you mean seriously to tell me that you actually believe that Truman can be nominated and elected to the United States Senate?"

Aylward said he could.

The boss told the chairman and Jim to ask Truman.

At that moment the judge was in the so-called outstate. The word had, and still has, a special Missouri meaning, in that it represents the entire state save for the metropolises in the state's east and west. It has been said that Missouri, like all Gaul, is divided into three parts, the two cities and the country, or outstate, area.

When the word came, the judge was speaking in thirty-five counties for a statewide $10 million bond issue for improving the penal and eleemosynary institutions. He was staying at the Osage Hotel in Warsaw. Rooms in this hostelry were two dollars per day, and meals fifty cents. The proprietors, Mr. and Mrs. Elbert Edwards, served family style, and told guests to "Pitch until you win." The dining room was in the basement, with seats for seventy-five people.

Chicken was served three times a week and always on Sunday. Truman took the Kansas City call on the wall phone in the lobby, and was told to go to the Terry Hotel in Sedalia. There the two Jims asked him to run.

The judge was as surprised by the request, which he knew came from Pendergast, as was Park when told he was to be governor. With little hesitation he accepted. That evening a resident of Sedalia, Frank Monroe, entertained him, and the judge duly displayed the reluctance that a candidate should show. He told Monroe he did not aspire to the office of senator at that time, for to step aside from the office of collector would be "too great a sacrifice from the business standpoint," but he did say "that I knew what a good organization man he was," and if when he got back home it was decided it was best for the party for him to run, he would do so.[21]

That summer of 1934 the primary race was between three candidates. In addition to Truman there was a congressman from Richmond, north of Kansas City, Jacob L. "Tuck" Milligan, brother of the federal attorney Maurice Milligan, who if elected would be Clark's man. A third was Congressman John J. Cochran of St. Louis, whom Truman believed to be the candidate of the anti-Pendergast *Post-Dispatch*. By all accounts Cochran was an excellent man, the state's leading congressman. Crippled, with one leg, he was a dedicated, attractive candidate.

Aylward carefully organized Truman's campaign. He opened it with a rally in Columbia to impress the intellectuals at the University of Missouri and people in what he described as the surrounding Bible Belt. He brought in Truman supporters from Jefferson City thirty miles away, "all those job holders," and transported other enthusiasts from St. Louis and Kansas City.[22] He put the Pendergast candidate through a grueling schedule, sending him (to use Truman's own description) "from town to town and from County to County and from daylight until midnight," two to ten appearances a day.[23] The candidate believed he shook hands with one hundred thousand people. Aylward arranged for the writing of speeches and sent them by courier, Truman's friend Fred Canfil—who was to figure in larger ways in Truman's campaign for renomination in 1940. He released them in advance to reporters who did not have to listen to them. One time when Canfil failed to connect with the candidate, Truman improvised and reporters wrote their stories from advance copies. The editor at the *Post-Dispatch* was furious, thinking himself outwitted, and perhaps partly out of his paper's animus for Truman told Aylward that he never would print another speech or portions thereof. Aylward pleaded with him, promised it never would happen again, and the editor relented.

For Truman the campaign was exhausting. The summer was hot, the hottest on record, with temperatures over one hundred degrees on twenty-one days, surpassing the previous record of sixteen days in 1901. Aylward remembered corn burning up in the fields, with the grasshoppers eating what was left. There were no leaves on it—"you could even smell it burning from the highway."[24]

Gradually Truman's attraction to voters became evident, for the presiding judge of Jackson County had much to recommend him. He was no orator, and read his canned speeches as fast as he could, to get them over with. If his voice was acceptable in Missouri, its singsong put hundreds of people to sleep—a Missouri country voice was nothing less than a lullaby. But his connections were impeccable, just as Aylward told Pendergast: Masonry, the Baptist church, war service (he had attended every annual state convention of the American Legion). He had been president of the Missouri County Judge Association, and because Missouri has 114 counties this meant support of 342 judges. He had communicated his concern for roads to all of them. Because he had taken part in planning for the Kansas City area that included several counties, even Johnson County in Kansas, he knew all the state legislators and state senators; he had organized a state planning board. It was true that the state's two major newspapers, the *Post-Dispatch* and the equally anti-Pendergast *Kansas City Star*, had hydrophobia, as he put it, every time they mentioned him. After the campaign he concluded they told so many lies that people in a great many counties where they circulated voted for him.

Senator Clark announced that the Pendergast candidate was "conducting a campaign of mendacity and imbecility unparalleled in the history of Missouri."[25] People just laughed. They knew that in the state's annals this was exaggeration.

Governor Park came out for him. He wrote an inquirer that "While I shall not take the stump for Judge Truman, he is my neighbor and long time friend and naturally I will vote for him. He is a high-class, Christian gentleman."[26]

More to the point was the candidate's machine support. It is possible, as Cochran claimed, that the St. Louis congressman's own prediction that he, Cochran, would receive 125,000 votes in St. Louis persuaded Pendergast to up his own vote for Truman. To ensure against misbehavior from St. Louis, Pendergast could marshal tens of thousands of ghost votes. Something evidently did happen, as Pendergast had a problem in St. Louis and he was no man to ignore a problem. In St. Louis's fourth ward Cochran received 5,568 votes, Milligan 18, and Truman 8. In the St. Louis area Cochran received less than he predicted, 104,265 votes, while Truman tallied 3,742. Pendergast had to, and did, make up for all this. In twenty-seven heavily Democratic precincts in Kansas City's north side Truman received 13,450 votes, Cochran 17. In Jackson County, Truman received 120,180 votes to Cochran's 1,221.

But a close student of the election has written that it was not the machine vote but that of the outstate that brought victory. Statewide, Truman had 276,850, Cochran 236,105, Milligan 147,614. If one did not count Kansas City–Jackson County and St. Louis–St. Louis County votes, presuming cheating in both metropolises, Truman would have won, 134,707 to Cochran's 113,532 and Milligan's 128,401.[27]

The election in November against the Republican incumbent, Patterson, whose sole claim to fame in the Senate was the Lindbergh or Federal Kidnaping Act, passed after the kidnaping and death of the infant son of Charles and Anne Lindbergh in 1930, was not difficult. With an unerring instinct for oblivion, Patterson centered his campaign against President Roosevelt, stressing totalitarian dictatorship, loss of the free enterprise system, and communism.

A dinner was held for the senator-elect and family in the Christian Church of Independence shortly before the Trumans left for Washington, during which the townspeople celebrated their new national leader by enumerating his virtues. Among speakers that evening was the postmistress at Marceline, Anne Watson, who told Truman, to the amusement of the audience, "Someday you will be elected President and I will be there to see you inaugurated." Reportedly he laughed louder than the whole crowd put together.[28]

For Truman to receive election to the Senate only a few months after believing, with excellent reason, that his political days were over, was a heady experience. Celebrating at the Christian Church, surrounded by friends and supporters, he enjoyed himself thoroughly. For Pendergast, however, the senatorial election had purposes other than providing a faithful member of the machine with an office. It brought the machine to its highest point of influence. It persuaded Senator Clark to cooperate with Pendergast rather than skewer him. Clark was coming up for reelection in 1938 and needed support from the man who took over Kansas City after its citizens voted for reform, elected most of the congressmen after a Republican governor vetoed the Democratic gerrymanders, elected Governor Park, and sent Truman to the Senate. Victory for the man of Independence brought Clark to the boss's side. This in turn allowed Pendergast to obtain all the jobs allotted Missouri under the New Deal's work relief program, the Works Progress Administration. The choice of a state's WPA administrator lay with its senators. Early in 1935, Truman and Clark chose a loyal machine member, Matthew S. Murray of Kansas City. Murray controlled eighty thousand jobs. Thereafter when citizens wrote Governor Park requesting help in finding WPA employment, the governor told them to get in touch with Murray, who was "in complete charge of Federal work relief in Missouri." When they wrote Senator Truman, he advised, "If you will send us endorsements from the Kansas City Democratic Organization, I shall be glad to do what I can for you."[29]

2

Collapse of the Machine

T he principal problem that confronted Senator Truman during his first term in Washington, apart from his Senate responsibilities, was his connection with the Pendergast machine. Truman was Pendergast's protégé. He hence was vulnerable to any antagonist who managed to diminish or perhaps even end the power of his mentor. It was true that Pendergast had reached a veritable apogee of power in the mid-1930s, and to any observer it might well have appeared that the walls of his Kansas City fortress and those of his supporters garrisoned in Jefferson City and of his congressional delegation—two senators, and most of his state's members of the House of Representatives—were too formidable to be breached. But the man who was known as the boss was into his sixties and could not last forever. Questions of succession were arising. Times were changing, the Rooseveltian New Deal was in course, and it was a brave new world in American politics as well as in society and economics. People everywhere were wondering how long machine politics could continue, whether time was about to catch up with the several machines in the large eastern and midwestern cities and the southern satrapy of Memphis presided over by Boss Ed Crump. Truman, it seemed, had chosen to be part of an anachronism, and could turn out to be a one-term senator in Washington.

The individual who destroyed Pendergast, and in the course of the destruction undertook to obtain Truman's Senate seat, was Lloyd Stark, who became governor of Missouri upon the end of Guy B. Park's four-year term. Tall, thin-faced, straight-mouthed, with chiseled features and hair combed down, Stark had been a successful businessman as general manager and chairman of the board of Stark Brothers Nurseries and Orchards Company. He had presided over the large nursery in Louisiana, Missouri, north of St. Louis, established in 1816 by his great-grandfather, James H. Stark. In 1893 the founder's grandson, Clarence Stark, bought a new variety of apple in Peru, Iowa, and named it Stark's Red Delicious. In 1914 the governor's brother Paul had gone to West Virginia and found an apple tree high on the side of a hill that bore remarkable yellow apples. The brother bought the tree, built a steel cage around it, and took some scions to Missouri—"Stark's Golden Delicious" apples. In addition to managing the nursery, Lloyd Stark could boast military experience. He graduated from Annapolis in 1908 and served four years in the navy. Acquiring a reserve commission as captain in the field artillery, he received promotion to major during the World War, and afterward was addressed as Major Stark. He was very ambitious politically. He sought the governorship in 1932, and Pendergast twice refused it, first by siding with Wilson, afterward giving it to Park; a *Post-Dispatch* photograph showed Stark and Pendergast at Wilson's funeral confronting each other, Pendergast almost visibly saying no.[1] Stark made his third try in 1936, succeeded, and soon after his election turned against Pendergast. One suspects he might have sought the seat of Senator Clark, who was up for reelection in 1938, except that Clark was such a good stump speaker that the governor perhaps decided to wait until 1940 and deal with a senator easier to defeat. Clark's seat also opened a year before the collapse of the machine.

1

At the beginning of Truman's work in the Senate, the new member of the upper house did his best to be recognized as a senator in good standing and not the gentleman from Pendergast. He had just begun to make his way when the Pendergast cloud again descended. A scandal over vote frauds broke out in Kansas City.

Senator Truman's initial experiences in Washington were hardly encouraging. He was unacquainted with the city, beyond a few trips he had made over the years. His first trip to the East Coast, other than passing in and out of New York City during and after the war, was in 1928 when he addressed the annual convention of the Daughters of the American Revolution in Washington. He seems to have entered and departed without fanfare, for he never mentioned the trip again. The next year he reappeared in the nation's capital to dedicate a monument as president of the National Old Trails Association, a group that promoted national roads along routes of the eighteenth- and nineteenth-century trails. During his last years as presiding judge he went to Washington a few times in his role as reemployment director for Missouri. These were his experiences when he reappeared in the city as a senator, to endure the unpleasant task of annually seeking out an apartment for the family, especially unpleasant because of the need, he felt, to discover low-rent apartments. The resultant conditions of life were not nearly as agreeable as those to which he was accustomed in Independence. In his hometown he lived in a seventeen-room Victorian house with a spacious lawn. In Washington it was a forgettable series of two-bedroom apartments fronting neighboring flats or the street, hot and noisy in summers if he stayed in them, or else nondescript hotel rooms with meals taken in their dining rooms.

In his initial period in Washington he felt so out of place, coming from Missouri. He wrote an army friend, "It is rather lonesome here in Washington, when you don't know anybody, and I'd like very much to see a lot of people with a western viewpoint. Most of the people in this town think the western boundary of the United States is the Allegheny Mountains."[2]

The senator's first days and months were depressing. He once said that he came to the Senate as "timid as a country boy on the campus of a great university."[3] He was treated as such. In the Senate chamber he received a desk in the last row. In the Senate office building his suite consisted of three rooms on the second floor, looking out on the grass-covered inner court. As he sat at his distant desk in the chamber or worked in the suite, he received little attention from colleagues, who save for two or three decent human beings ignored him. Carl A.

Hatch of New Mexico and Sherman H. Minton of Indiana, both freshmen senators, shared their timidities. Among senators with seniority only Burton K. Wheeler of Montana and Hamilton Lewis of Illinois took interest in their Missouri colleague. Wheeler was a maverick and frequently at odds with the Roosevelt administration; the president cordially hated him. Truman was grateful for Wheeler's friendship, and wrote a senator when he himself was president that Wheeler's viewpoint "is almost opposite to mine but you must understand that sixteen years ago Burt Wheeler was one of the few Senators in the Senate who was in any way decent to the junior Senator from Missouri and I can't forget that. . . . I shall continue to like him as long as I live."[4] Ham Lewis also became a favorite, especially after the Illinois senator told him, "Harry, don't you go to the Senate with an inferiority complex. You sit there about six months, and you wonder how you got there. And after that you wonder how the rest of them got there."

Meeting the president required five or six months. Truman was much impressed: "He was as cordial and nice to me as he could be. It was quite an event for a country boy to go calling on the President of the United States." But the experience displayed his unimportance. He told an interviewer long afterward, when he had thought it over, that the trouble was Pendergast: "I was under a cloud."[5] His administrative assistant, Victor R. Messall, accompanied him to the executive offices behind the White House, and when the two of them got to the desk of the president's appointments secretary and were seated outside the president's office, they found Secretary of Agriculture Henry A. Wallace and other cabinet members including Secretary of the Interior Harold L. Ickes sitting around on sofas and chairs and talking with each other. None of the cabinet members acknowledged the presence of the senator, who waited in silence. At last the appointments secretary told Truman he could go in to see the president. The interview was for fifteen minutes, and the senator came out in seven.

From the way he was treated during the initial Senate years Truman later remembered a saying of the humorist of the post–Civil War era, Josh Billings. He would not have applied it to the sophisticated president of the United States, who was pleasant to him, however dismissive. It held for the cabinet members who gave him no attention, especially Wallace and Ickes, whom Truman as president would dismiss from his own cabinet. It assuredly applied to the senators who ignored him when he first came to Washington. Billings in *Trump Kards* (1877) advised, "Dont dispize yure poor relashuns, they may bekum suddenly ritch, and then it will be awkward to explain things to them."

Two years after the initial interview with the president, the senator began to discern how impressed Roosevelt had been with him. The occasion was the remarkable contest in the Senate that year, 1937, over the choice of a majority leader. A delegation of senators had just returned from Arkansas, where they had attended the funeral of Joseph T. Robinson, who had been the leader, and on the way back there was much discussion as to his successor. A contest had arisen between Alben W. Barkley of Kentucky and Pat Harrison of Mississippi. President Roosevelt wanted Barkley, who seemed more amenable to presidential instruction. FDR was extremely sensitive to Senate leadership at this time, for he had just launched his campaign to reorganize (or "pack," his enemies said) the Supreme Court and was encountering opposition everywhere, not least in the Senate.

Truman admired both of the contestants, Barkley and Harrison, but promised his vote to the latter, and the president in a show of disdain for the Missouri senator had Jim Farley call Pendergast and ask that Truman change his vote to Barkley. The boss, who at this time was in Colorado Springs, called Truman. Pendergast told Truman he would like him to change if possible but that it was no large concern to him and Truman should make the decision. Irritated at being treated as the senator from Pendergast, that the president through an intermediary would take the great circle route, Washington to Colorado Springs to Washington, when a simple phone call to the senator in the capital would have sufficed, Truman voted for Harrison. Knowing that the presidential effort to push him around would become public, he took the precaution of showing his ballot, marked for Harrison, to a colleague, Clyde L. Herring of Iowa, before casting it. The president, let it be added, won the contest to make Barkley majority leader by obtaining the vote of William H. Dieterich of Illinois, and employed the same crude method he sought to use on Truman. He asked Farley to telephone Dieterich. Farley refused, but someone, either FDR's intimate Harry L. Hopkins or the lawyer Thomas G. Corcoran, did. The threat to Dieterich was that

WPA funds for Chicago where the Roosevelt supporter and head of the city machine, Edward J. Kelly, was mayor, were at stake. Barkley won by Dieterich's single vote.[6]

During these experiences in Washington, Truman was discovering that relations with Lloyd Stark were up and down in a disconcerting way. As he felt like a country boy in the Senate and meeting Roosevelt, and was treated like a country boy by most of the senators and the president, so he became uneasy as to what Stark was doing or about to do.

At first his relations with Stark were unexceptionable, for the man who became Pendergast's nemesis and Truman's bitter enemy was as friendly as he could be. When Stark sought the governorship the third time he begged Truman and Clark to recommend him to Pendergast, and the two senators went to the length of escorting him from Washington to New York to see Pendergast, who was either coming into New York or about to leave it on one of his European trips. Pendergast's welcome was suitable for the occasion, meeting the almost obvious candidate to replace Governor Park, whose single four-year term under the Missouri constitution was coming to an end. After showing himself to the boss Stark discreetly retired to another room, while Pendergast unbeknownst to him protested to the senators, who continued enthusiastically to recommend him. "I don't like the son of a bitch," the boss said. "He's a no good son of a bitch."[7] Pendergast gave in, seeing that Stark possessed state prominence and military experience. He would have support from St. Louis because of the proximity of Louisiana, and support from Kansas City if the boss went along. Pendergast advised him to attempt some outstate support. On the train back to Washington, Truman was embarrassed, he wrote his wife, because in the compartment Stark insisted upon hugging and virtually kissing him, he said, in appreciation of what the senators had done.

Receiving the endorsement, Stark in 1936 easily took the nomination in the primary and won election the following November. Truman did everything he could, writing Stark, "Whenever I can be of any service in any way whatever, all you need to do is to indicate it, and I will be right there." He acclaimed Stark's campaign as a harbinger of great things, at one point sending a telegram that read, "This is a forerunner of Missouri's greatest administration." Stark informed a close Truman confederate, knowing word would get back, that "Of course, you know that Harry is one of the best friends I have in the world . . ."[8]

After the governor took office everything became uncertain. On February 1, Senator Truman informed his wife that he had seen the governor, who was most cordial. Stark was showing independence, would do what he pleased, "and so would I if I were in his shoes." But "I really believe he'll make one of Missouri's real ones. Anyway he's not a booze fighter nor is he running after the ladies. So if we don't get jobs for the faithful, maybe the state will profit anyway. He likes pomp and circumstance and maybe that's all there is to any of it."[9] Not long afterward, on March 11, Stark was showing a certain duplicity, although not directed at Truman. He wrote the senator and enclosed a separate note: "On anything you are vitally and personally interested in, please pin a little note to the sheet of paper; otherwise, I will assume that you wrote it as a matter of politics. L.C.S."[10] That year the governor showed more duplicity. Truman spoke with his fellow legislator in the House of Representatives, the retired Kansas City boss Joe Shannon, who warned him, if somewhat pleasantly. "He says," Truman informed Bess, "Stark will run against Clark and not against me." Unsure of what was going on, Truman applied to Farley, who understood such things; Farley assured him that the Roosevelt administration would not help the governor against either Clark or Truman. The junior senator intended to go all the way to be sure Farley's words were reliable. "I hope he was speaking for the White House, but you never can tell. I'm to see F.D.R. when he gets back from Warm Springs."[11]

Things moved back and forth in relations with Stark. Truman took what he hoped would be measures to ensure that Clark would not become too friendly with the governor. "I've ended the Clark-Stark hookup," he reported to Bess on November 23, 1937. Simultaneously he picked up disconcerting talk about his reassurance from Farley. "It is rumored that Farley and the President are at outs, which won't help me any." So far, however, he believed, "I'm on top." A few days later he was convinced that Clark and Pendergast were together, against Stark and the president. In a letter of November 1, 1937, the governor asked him and his wife to stay at the governor's mansion at the first opportunity. "Maybe," he concluded in a letter to Bess, "he thinks that appeals to a country boy."[12]

During these distractions—his indifferent if not hostile reception in Washington, the uneasy relationship with the governor—there was another development, this time in Kansas City, where horrendous vote frauds during the November election of 1936 had come into view.

In the early era of the machine's history, and especially during the 1920s when Jim Aylward was chairman of the Jackson County Democratic Committee and beginning in 1923 the party's state chairman, the Pendergast machine made its way mostly because of superb organization. The individual responsible, Aylward, was an independent Democrat rather than a machine man; indeed he had been a Shannon supporter, a rabbit rather than a Pendergast goat, to use the Kansas City descriptions. He brought the Democratic factions together in the city election of 1926, electing a majority of the council under the revised charter. He held no public office. He was a protégé and law partner of Kansas City's most prominent attorney, Frank P. Walsh, who during the World War was a national figure as co-chairman, with former president William H. Taft, of the National Labor Board. After the war Walsh established law offices in New York and Washington and did not return to Kansas City, instead leaving his younger partner in charge. After the Democratic triumph in the city, Aylward built the organization into a highly efficient group, bringing it to the "zenith of its power."[13] He had seventy-five hundred workers directly interested in winning elections for the party, ten or twelve to a precinct, and they were not all job holders, for the machine did not have that many jobs. Under Aylward the Democrats set up a registration department and a polling department. The latter polled every householder, every voter in the community. When a machine member was unsure of a householder's politics he put that individual in the Republican column. "So that we actually had a substantial, accurate, truthful poll, and, as I say, it covered the entire city and most of the county—the townships out in the county. We had that kind of a working organization."[14] For elections Aylward had a speakers' committee. There even was a habeas corpus committee, which cared for members of the organization arrested for some alleged violation of the law that was only a device to get them off the streets during campaigns. Until home rule came in for the city police department in 1932, the police were under the control of whoever was governor in Jefferson City; throughout the 1920s and down to the installation of Governor Park in 1933, Missouri's governors were Republicans.

During the early period of the machine and in the 1920s there undoubtedly was some cheating at the polls. Machines across the country did it as a matter of course. The boss's older brother, Alderman Jim, disdained cheating; he said he did not need it. One cannot be sure whether if confronted by necessity he might have cheated. Boss Tom would and did, but most of it seems to have been occasional shenanigans in the first and second wards of the city, his home territory, wards that fronted on the Missouri River and contained the city's poorest inhabitants.

What appears to have happened is that after the boss gained control of the city and county and his power reached to the statehouse and both houses of Congress, he found more compelling reasons for cheating. When he raised his sights to state and national power he needed to offset St. Louis, where the ward bosses, he thought, were cheating. He also had to offset the outstate, which was culturally removed from him and his city friends, or gain its support with candidates such as Truman.

Gradually, too, the convenience of cheating, an easy thing to do, overwhelmed what scruples Pendergast had. Machine members accustomed themselves to cheat, and in the November election of 1936 they threw caution to the winds and brought in vote totals in eccentric proportion to Kansas City's population. The first ward, with a population of 19,923, cast 20,687 votes. In the second there were similar results. In 1925 that ward cast 3,338 Democratic votes. Without any increase in population, ghost voting became evident in 1930 when the number of voters doubled to 6,128. It rose to 15,940 in 1934 when the machine's mayoral candidate carried the ward by 13,721. In 1936, President Roosevelt received 88 percent of 21,242 votes in that ward. That year Pendergast's statehouse nominee, Stark, received 19,202, his opponent 12. The population of the second ward—men, women, and children—was 18,478. In the election of 1936 precinct captains and heelers showed almost no willingness to be careful, to spread addresses: at 912 Tracy Street a house contained 141 registered voters, at 700 Main Street, 112 voters lived in a vacant lot. On the day of that election spooks, sleepers, and riders appeared everywhere. The dead were easiest to vote. "Now is the time," someone said, "for all good cemeteries to come to the aid of the party." Sleepers once resided in their precincts but moved, their names remaining on lists. Riders rode the range of precincts, leaving their brands on ballots in every corral.

In 1936 the population of Kansas City was 415,000, and the Census Bureau estimated that across the country only 60 percent of the population was over twenty-one, meaning that approximately 249,000 Kansas Citians would have been of voting age. In that group were persons too ill or feeble to register. Others were in prison or were aliens or otherwise not entitled to vote. A registration of 200,000 in Kansas City would have been large, representing nearly half the population. The books for that year showed 268,000 names, 64.5 percent of the city's population. The Republican candidate for governor in 1936, Jesse W. Barrett, analyzed the reason for his defeat by Stark:

> I see my total vote has gone to 772,000. No Republican ever got that much before except Caulfield. He received 784,000 and we called it a great landslide. Hyde was elected by 720,000. Sam Baker's vote was only 640,000, yet it was sufficient to elect. The Democrats just dug up a lot of votes from some place and that is what overwhelmed me.[15]

The reason for overexertion by the machine in 1936 was probably the absence of Pendergast until mid-September, because of a heart attack suffered the second day of the Democratic national convention in Philadelphia, which opened on June 23. He had gone down from New York, where he was staying on the twenty-ninth floor of the Waldorf, and met Senator Truman; the two posed for a picture with a group of politicians including Aylward and Farley. Boss Tom wore his hat, covering his nearly bald head, and was smiling and in excellent spirits. He returned to the hotel that night, did not feel well, and next day was found to be suffering from a coronary thrombosis and was hospitalized. Weeks later, recovering and still in New York, he suffered an abdominal blockage caused by a cancerous growth, requiring an operation. He returned to Kansas City on a private railway car and entered Menorah Hospital for another operation in which he was fitted with a colostomy.

But one cannot be certain of what caused the overzealousness. It may have been not so much Pendergast's absence as his turning to other concerns, for two years earlier his fascination with betting on horse races had changed into a mania in which he placed bets every afternoon and listened to the races by three direct wires from his Main Street office. One of his lawyers later explained how horse races affected him:

> He told me that when the afternoon was here, 2:30, 3 o'clock, he would go into a little room, and there he would take the form sheet, and with the advice of a friend of his he would handicap these horses, and then he would sit with the telephone at his ear and he would hear a call, "They're at the post." Later, "They're off," and so over that telephone, by ear and not by eye, he watched those horses run to the finish line—all the thrill that can ever come to any man, for that which possesses him and which he cannot down.[16]

He soon was wagering big money. A sound tip on a long-shot horse apparently was his undoing, for he won nearly a quarter of a million dollars on a single race. He began to try to beat that record and scattered ten-thousand-dollar bets over the country. As government figures would show, he wagered $2 million in 1935 and lost $600,000.

The reporter for the *New York Times*, Arthur Krock, explained the machine's exertions in 1936 by a simple effort of captains and heelers to increase their totals to make themselves look good in the eyes of machine leaders. If someone in a neighboring precinct was bringing in a big vote, the course of wisdom was to surpass it. This despite the fact that it was unnecessary in 1936 when Roosevelt was leading the national ticket against the Republican candidate, the hapless governor of Kansas, Alf M. Landon. Roosevelt was going to bring victory to most Democrats that year.

In Kansas City the first ward's irregularities had their own explanation—it was home territory to the Pendergast dynasty, Alderman Jim and Boss Tom. The latter had moved away to Ward Parkway, and took it for granted that the family bailiwick would continue to bring in whatever vote totals he needed. He perhaps did not watch his workers there as carefully as he might, had he been in residence.

In the second ward the trouble may have been Pendergast's lieutenant, an old rival named Casimir J. Welch. In the mid-1920s, Cas Welch joined the machine rather than fighting it, and Pendergast subcontracted the ward to him. It contained many black voters, whom Welch dealt fairly with. But without much attention from headquarters he raised his totals during the late 1920s and early

1930s. In 1934 the leader of the National Youth Movement, Joe Fennelly, watched machine workers mobilize hundreds of pads, as ghost voters were known generically. They lined them up, each with a slip of paper bearing the name under which he was to vote, and marched them through the voting place. When the line emerged, the voters exchanged hats, received new slips bearing new names, and filed back in again. It was estimated that Welch in 1936 (he died in April of that year) was probably voting fifteen thousand pads.[17]

On October 8, 1936, a lawyer and head of the Citizens League of Kansas City, Fred E. Whitten, went to Jefferson City and told Governor Park of evidence that the registration lists were padded. The governor refused to act. He said it was Republican propaganda, and that if there was anything to justify an investigation he of course would take action.

After the election a federal judge in the city, Albert L. Reeves, rose in wrath. Years before, in 1918, the judge had had personal experience with the Pendergast machine. He ran for Congress in Kansas City and ever afterward believed he was counted out. Defeated by twelve thousand votes, he lost one precinct by a vote of 700 to 1; in this precinct thirty people voted up to the time the polls closed. Appointed to the federal bench by President Harding, Reeves was a Baptist Sunday school teacher, stern and austere. He impaneled a grand jury under an old post–Civil War statute that allowed federal intervention in local elections in cases where voters—it had been designed to protect black voters from the Ku Klux Klan—were denied the franchise or otherwise misrepresented at the polls. To be sure of impartiality he chose jurors from outside Kansas City. "Gentlemen," he told the group, "there is crying need for the purification of the ballot in America. . . . A corrupt vote may be likened to a loaded and cocked gun pointed at the very heart of America. . . . Gentlemen, reach for all, even if you find them in high authority. Move on them!"[18]

Reeves had the assistance of the federal district attorney, Maurice Milligan, brother of Congressman Tuck Milligan, who opposed Truman in the senatorial race of 1934. To Missouri's junior senator, Maurice Milligan was a blot on any occasion. Bennett Clark had sponsored him as a favor to his brother, during the time when Clark was opposing Pendergast. Truman reported to Bess that the federal attorney was a drunkard and a "libertine," whatever that meant. Years later, annotating a book that sought to evaluate Milligan's intelligence, Truman described him as a "dumb cluck."[19] Actually, as two recent writers have allowed, he was "an above average lawyer, not very ambitious."[20] His ability as a prosecutor he owed to two assistants, Randall W. Wilson and Sam C. Blair, who did all the heavy-duty trial work. Wilson was a courtroom strategist of rare ability. Blair drafted the vote-fraud indictments.

Inspired by the indignation of Judge Reeves, and with the help of Milligan and his assistants, the grand jury and subsequent trial juries, the latter similarly composed of residents outside of Jackson County, discovered the fraud that everyone in Kansas City knew about. The evidence was overwhelming. Missouri election laws required polls in cities such as Kansas City to remain open until seven o'clock in the evening. At one precinct a captain who was not even an election official at 4:30 p.m. turned the hands of the clock to 7:00 p.m. and closed the polling place, despite protests of voters in line. The captain did not even count votes cast but read from a memorandum in his hand the number of votes he wished to record, which was done. The first group of ballots the grand jury examined, sealed in sacks, showed ninety-five ballots changed from straight Republican to straight Democratic votes. In one precinct a polling place was a barbershop, and after the voting the machine's ballotsmiths took the ballot box to the basement, dumped its contents on a table, and calculated what had to be done. They found 113 ballots improperly marked for Republican candidates, requiring erasure and re-marking. When all was over one of the officials went upstairs, stretched out in a barber chair, and complained to a friend. "I am all in," he said. "Some of those damned Republicans marked their ballots so hard it was all I could do to rub them out."[21] Slowly the ghost-voter trials wound their way to verdicts. Two years were required to care for the precinct captains and workers who acted illegally. Reeves, Milligan and his assistants, and the juries brought in 278 defendants and obtained 259 convictions; there were nineteen dismissals for various reasons, but no one was acquitted.

A state election board appointed by the legislature under a Permanent Registration Law purged the Kansas City rolls of tens of thousands of names. Registration dropped from 270,000 in November 1936 to 216,000 in a city election in the spring of 1938. The board shared its work with surviving machine officials who themselves disposed of countless names by misplacing or losing polling lists.

For Senator Truman, by the end of 1937, the vote-fraud trials were almost too much, and if combined with other woes they were more than that. He had been having problems in Washington because of his Pendergast origins. Governor Stark, who earlier had been one of Truman's best friends in all the world, cooperated with Reeves's investigation through the state election board. Stark had asked Jim Pendergast to go to Jefferson City, look over a list of possible members for the four-man board, and check off names friendly to the machine. The governor appointed none of the seven individuals Jim checked. Truman on November 19, 1937, at the time he was asking Farley if the administration was about to support Stark against Clark and himself and received assurance it would not, inquired of the national chairman if the U.S. attorney general would appoint a district attorney in Missouri to succeed Milligan, whose four-year term was coming to an end early the next year. The senator said he did not want to submit a name unless an appointment was to be made. Farley discovered that the attorney general and the president were cold toward any change in the office.[22]

Not long afterward Truman made an egregious error in his political calculations, in regard to Milligan in particular, his senatorial colleagues and the administration in general. The president called him and asked him not to refuse Milligan a reappointment by describing him to his fellow senators with the fatal phrase that his reappointment would be "personally obnoxious." Roosevelt was displaying more disdain for Truman. Faced with a presidential call, the senator did the correct thing by giving his word that he would not employ the fatal phrase. Truman should have let the matter go that way, and when Milligan's name came up in the Senate on February 15, 1938, should have absented himself from the chamber, claiming urgent business in Missouri or any other place that crossed his mind. Instead he lost his temper and treated the Senate to a diatribe against Judge Reeves and gratuitously included Reeves's fellow judge in Kansas City, Merrill E. Otis. He said that a Democrat could not obtain justice in the courts of Reeves and Otis any more than a Jew could obtain justice in the courts of Adolf Hitler. He accused Milligan of taking fees from a referee in bankruptcy whom the judges appointed, which was true, although such a practice was not illegal. Subsequently, in midsummer of that year, the referee pleaded nolo contendere in four counts of income tax evasion and received a six-month jail sentence.

Judges Reeves and Otis disqualified themselves for the trial, and a federal judge from Nebraska took the case.

Contrary to the impression of his speech, the senator was not against Milligan because of the vote-fraud prosecutions, he said, and he proposed that Milligan receive appointment as a special prosecutor to complete them. He only believed that Milligan was incompetent. "The detail work and the actual trial of the vote fraud cases," Truman said, "have been done by Mr. Milligan's two able deputies and not by Mr. Milligan. If the district attorney's office was to have been rewarded for vote fraud prosecutions, by a reappointment, one of these able deputies should have been appointed."[23]

His fellow senators sat through this logical exercise in silence, save for Styles Bridges, Republican of Maine, who argued that Reeves and Otis were doing splendid work. Bennett Clark, whom Truman thought he had moved into support of Pendergast and himself, contended that as his own appointee Milligan was a good man. Upon the vote Truman opposed and his colleagues unanimously voted in favor.

After the senator's speech Judge Reeves defended himself, describing the outburst in the Senate as a speech of a man nominated by ghost votes, elected with ghost votes, and whose speech was probably written by ghostwriters.

Truman knew he had gone too far. A few days later he wrote Joseph H. Leib: "Replying to your inquiry, I will not be a candidate for reelection to the Senate, in view of my speech on the Senate floor on Tuesday." He followed with the comment: "This is a personal and confidential letter to you and I request that you do not publish it whatsoever." When two years later he decided to run he asked Leib to give back the letter. According to Leib, "He said he wouldn't run as long as I had that original." Leib sent it. "But he always sent you a copy of his letters and I held on to the copy. He forgot he gave one to me." Leib thoughtfully did not release the copy for publication until half a dozen years after Truman's death.[24]

2

Early in 1938 there was continuing trouble with the Pendergast connection. In fact, in 1938–1939 it became deep trouble, for just at the time when the vote fraud investigation began to give evidence of coming to an end, having failed to reach higher-ups in the machine, Governor Stark forced Roosevelt to turn against the boss and send him to the federal penitentiary at Leavenworth.

In the first months of Stark's moves against Pendergast, Senator Truman had little understanding of what the governor was about. He was working as hard as he could and had little time to think of what Stark was doing. Following the advice of Senator Carl Hayden of Arizona, he tried to be a workhorse rather than a show horse. He wrote his young daughter Margaret that

> It just takes work and more work to accomplish anything—and your dad knows it better than anyone. It's been my policy to do every job assigned to me just a little better than anyone else has done it. . . . It takes work to do anything well. Most people expect everything and do nothing to get it. That is why some people are leaders in society, in politics, in religion, on the stage and elsewhere and some just stand and cry that they haven't been treated fairly.

He told Margaret that "Lazy people never get anywhere in anything." The result of work, he informed her, was happiness and friends: "There are some who can win and make others happy by doing it, and some who make enemies. You can be one who wins and makes friends and it is so much happier that way."[25] After a slow start in the Senate his labors there took on importance, his position among his fellow senators rose markedly, and his colleagues came to appreciate his knowledge and judgment on issues in which he made himself expert, even if he was capable of a lapse of judgment over Milligan and, what they did not know, in the letter to Leib. For his rising stature in the upper house he also could thank Burt Wheeler, who put him on a committee to revise the nation's transportation system—railroads, barge traffic on rivers and canals and steamers on the lakes, the increasing use of trucks, and future use (it was becoming dimly visible) of airplanes. The senator made himself expert in the competing merits of the several types of carriers. He helped put together the Civil Aeronautics Act of 1938, the federal statute governing aviation until airplane traffic was deregulated in 1978. Eventually, albeit after the primary in 1940, he became co-sponsor of the Wheeler-Truman

Transportation Act of that year, which President Roosevelt signed with a flourish.

All the while, however, Pendergast was creating a situation that made the machine vulnerable to the faithless governor. The involvement that gave Stark his golden opportunity took its beginnings, it later became clear, in the boss's losses in horse races, which were mounting faster than he could afford despite income from the machine and from cement, construction, and liquor. Money from any source attracted Pendergast, and he saw a way in which he could make himself useful in settling a problem that had afflicted fire insurance companies in Missouri since the 1920s. One of his own men, the same Emmet O'Malley who desired to be postmaster of Kansas City, failing in that endeavor had gone into the insurance business, and in 1933 Governor Park appointed him state commissioner of insurance. It is possible that O'Malley, who looked like a chubby, bespectacled banker but was nothing of the sort, suggested the idea of a fire insurance settlement to Pendergast. It is more likely that the suggestion came from the boss himself.

Acting as mediator in the fire insurance matter loomed as a way to make money in a hurry, and Pendergast seized it. O'Malley got in touch with the president of the Missouri Insurance Agents' Association, Alphonsus L. McCormack of St. Louis, and worked out a deal. In 1922 a previous insurance commissioner had issued an order rolling back fire insurance rates by 15 percent, later modified to 10 percent. The companies involved went to court, eventually to the Supreme Court in Washington, and argued that the order was confiscatory, infringing on their constitutional rights. Losing the issue, they regrouped and raised their rates by 16 2/3 percent. Suing in both federal and state courts, the 234 companies involved managed an arrangement whereby they could collect the new rates but the excess would be impounded pending the outcome of the litigation. By the mid-1930s the money for companies that operated outside of Missouri amounted to $9 million; $2 million had accumulated for companies that operated only within the state. O'Malley's deal with McCormack was for both national and local companies, which would receive 80 percent of their impounded premiums, with the balance to go to policyholders. The arrangement was confirmed in Chicago on January 23 and March 28, 1935, and for his services Pendergast was to receive a bribe of $750,000.

Curiously, if the boss had reported his bribe money as income he would have been home free, for he would have been assisting an arrangement and obtaining a fee therefor. Doubtless he did not think he needed to report it. Moreover, the reporting would have become known and would not have obtained good newspaper press in Missouri, as the arrangement was too favorable to the companies at expense of insured persons in Missouri. (A double standard doubtless was in place, for the well-known Missouri lawyer John T. Barker, who was engaged by the state to negotiate an arrangement and consented to the O'Malley arrangement, received a fee for protecting insured persons in Missouri, taken out of the insurance companies' award, of $423,606.)

In its negotiations the O'Malley-McCormack deal was complicated, but Chicago meetings involving Pendergast ensured a series of payments totaling $460,500 (the companies never paid the full amount), from which O'Malley received $62,500 and McCormack $82,500. Settlement of the matter became known as the Second Missouri Compromise. In the first, that of 1821, Missouri entered the Union, a move that led, after forty years, to the Civil War. In the second, Boss Tom Pendergast brought the machine in Kansas City to its collapse.

The details of the intricate arrangement need not concern the reader, save that where the deal came apart was in collecting and distributing the bribes to Pendergast and his two assistants. Collection from the companies lay with Charles R. Street, vice president of the Chicago branch of the Great American Insurance Company of New York, with whom Pendergast consented to the arrangement. Street earlier had represented the insurance companies in negotiation with the authorities in Missouri over how to handle the impounded money. The bribe money was to be in cash, impossible to trace. Street used the leading firm of fire insurance attorneys in the United States, a Chicago firm, Hicks and Folonie, to collect the money. When Ernest H. Hicks died in 1935, the Bureau of Internal Revenue made a routine check of his estate early in 1936 and discovered $100,500 for which the deceased had not paid income tax. Hicks's partner, Robert J. Folonie, averred that the firm was only an agent and had given the money to Street. The latter said he too was an agent and refused to relate to whom he passed the money. Street did write a note on May 4, 1936 (why he did it is unsure, the presumption being that he was seeking to get the BIR to close its investigation by bringing up the name of a major Democratic figure) that he was going on a short trip and upon return would go to Missouri. Meanwhile, he related, he could do nothing until the *Queen Mary* came in. The Chicago agent of the BIR, knowing the liner was making its maiden voyage and would arrive in New York on June 1, checked the passenger list and discovered the names of Mr. and Mrs. Thomas J. Pendergast.

By May 1936 it was clear from the disbursing agent, Street, that Pendergast had taken a bribe, but other things were unclear. The extent of the bribe evidently was more than $100,500, and rumor in Missouri had it that a bribe to someone, not necessarily Pendergast, amounted to 5 percent of the impounded money paid in to the national companies, that is, $500,000. Street as disbursing agent was not talking, and when the BIR's Chicago office on March 7, 1937, issued a summons, he showed up the next day and said no more, save he had filed an amended tax return for the year 1935 and included the $100,500 as income and paid additional taxes of $47,093 plus interest of $2,825.60. He managed this delay, to be sure, because citizens were allowed a year after their regular tax payments to file amended returns. The Chicago office of the BIR apparently had no more recourse than to wait another year and see if Street would declare the presumably much larger additional amount of the bribe and pay taxes and interest on it. Presumption had to be that he would not, as it would be too much money, $400,000. Street thoughtfully died on February 1, 1938, closing off any possibility of more response from him.

At this juncture it was none other than Pendergast who ruined everything for himself and his assistants. After his illness and surgery in New York in 1936 he had gone to Kansas City and was in Menorah Hospital and needed $10,000, or so he told McCormack. Why this sum is impossible to know; it surely could not have been for his bill at Menorah, for this was the era of small medical costs. If it were gambling debts, this too was unlikely, for he could have bet $10,000 on a single race. Considering the payments that preceded, it was not much: McCormack already had made three trips to give him $50,000, $50,000, and $330,000. (Checks collected from fourteen large companies by Street for the first two payments totaled $100,500, and Street kept $500.) Street sent the $10,000 by telegram to the First National Bank of St. Louis, and instructed the bank to give cash to McCormack—and thereby, when a BIR agent two years later discovered a carbon of the telegram, identified McCormack as an intermediary. The BIR asked McCormack what happened to the money and he said he lost it at a racetrack and gave the date. An agent checked the date and discovered the track had closed two weeks earlier. McCormack, who had been making his points by himself, asked for a lawyer. For a while he held out, but the pressure to talk became unbearable. It is not clear what happened— by this time it was March of 1939—between him and executives of the large companies that provided most of the bribe money, whom the federal attorney, Milligan, summoned to Kansas City, except that the possibility of McCormack's going to jail must have combined with that of criminal prosecution of the executives, one of whom was heard to say, "We cannot afford to be indicted in a hick town like Kansas City."[26] The result was a plea bargain whereby McCormack identified Pendergast as recipient of most of the money, with O'Malley and himself receiving smaller shares.

The role of Governor Stark in the negotiations in Chicago and Kansas City was at the outset small. Stark became governor only on January 1, 1937. Nor did anyone, other than the principals, have knowledge of what was going on until May 1936, after Hicks died and the BIR made its routine check, and Hicks's partner identified Street and the latter indulged in ruminations about going to Missouri and the arrival of the *Queen Mary*. Even then, Street held out for nearly another year, until, faced with the March 15 deadline and the summons, he paid taxes on the first installments of the bribe and made them a private matter. All Stark could observe from Jefferson City, once he was in office, was that Emmet O'Malley seemed unduly close to Pendergast.

The vote fraud investigation brought Stark into opposition to the Kansas City boss. After an act by the state legislature he appointed the election board to purge the Kansas City rolls. To that board he refused to appoint a single Pendergast nominee. In the summer of 1937 he took a vacation cruise to Alaska, aboard a U.S. Navy ship, a voyage that perhaps he arranged because he was a graduate of the Naval Academy. The governor's wife and children were spending the summer at Woods Hole in Massachusetts. At that time Pendergast was vacationing in Colorado Springs, at the Broadmoor Hotel, in the top tower suite that cost fifty-five dollars per day, exclusive of meals. It was a spacious hostelry in the town that had been an

American spa for decades—Harry Truman's aunt had gone there, although not to the Broadmoor, in the 1890s. The boss was not at ease in Colorado Springs, and peremptorily asked Stark to stop off and talk with him on the way back to Missouri, which Stark did. During their two-hour summit meeting the governor told Pendergast he would do nothing to stop the vote fraud investigation. The name of O'Malley came up, and Pendergast asked Stark to continue O'Malley in office for another four-year term. The boss seemed strangely sensitive about O'Malley, an unpopular figure as insurance commissioner because he had criticized the insurance programs of the fraternal orders, such as the Woodmen of the World, Odd Fellows, and Maccabees. It was estimated that in the election of 1936 he had cost the Democrats tens of thousands of votes. The governor told Pendergast that O'Malley's days as commissioner were numbered, but he could remain for a while as a holdover, depending upon good behavior. It may have been out of desire to strike at Pendergast that Stark refused to continue O'Malley, or on account of rumors about the Second Missouri Compromise.

Soon the governor was making another point against Pendergast. A year and more earlier, on February 1, 1936, a federal court, three judges sitting, the two Kansas City district judges and Circuit Judge Kimbrough Stone, had accepted the insurance compromise so far as it applied to the national companies. In March 1937 Stark appointed a young St. Louis lawyer, James M. Douglas, to a vacancy on the state supreme court, and in the autumn of that year the court in a 4–3 decision, Douglas voting with the majority, rejected the compromise for the $2 million in money impounded for companies that operated only within Missouri. One must suppose that Governor Stark, despite the impropriety, inquired of Douglas, before appointing him, concerning his sentiments toward the impending insurance settlement. He would not have missed the opportunity. The issue at once became controversial. When Douglas came up for nomination in the primary in August 1938, Pendergast sponsored a circuit judge against him, while Stark marshaled St. Louis and the outstate. Douglas won by 119,485 votes, this though he lost Jackson County by 88,926 votes.

In the summer of 1937, as an editorial writer for the *Post-Dispatch* remarked later, "History began to hum." The newspaperman recalled that early in 1937, "As Governor, Stark was moving along the beaten path of colorless regularity. But that summer afternoon at Colorado Springs changed everything."[27] After the Stark-Pendergast conference both antagonists talked freely to reporters. Pendergast told a *Post-Dispatch* reporter that he would have consented to the retirement of O'Malley, had it not been for an editorial in the paper he interpreted as calling for a test between Stark and himself. The test came in October when the governor told O'Malley not to argue for the insurance compromise before the Missouri Supreme Court. O'Malley defied the governor, who fired him. The former insurance commissioner described Stark as a polecat. Pendergast made O'Malley director of Kansas City's water department, singularly appropriate. Pendergast issued a statement concerning his erstwhile friend the governor: "I ask no quarter and will give no quarter." About this time he was heard privately to describe the governor as "an apple-knocking son of a bitch."[28]

Calculating friends and enemies, the boss of Kansas City could sense that Roosevelt was not supporting him with the fervor the president should have shown. It was not any act of presidential commission so much as the omissions. As a Roosevelt-before-Chicago man, the boss would have been worthy of respect. Whatever happened at the Chicago convention, after the inauguration the president showered Pendergast with patronage. But during the Stark-Pendergast contretemps that was turning into an open row, Roosevelt put no pressure on the governor. Pendergast at Colorado Springs reminded the president, through an interview with the *Post-Dispatch* reporter, that such behavior was improper. "Nationally," the reporter wrote, "Pendergast has not joined in the Democratic chorus of praise for President Roosevelt, but has refrained from comment. He dislikes what he calls 'personal opportunists' and prefers men who are loyal to their organizations." The boss's "closest personal and political national connection," Pendergast told his Boswell, was Postmaster General Farley.[29]

It is possible that the boss's refusal to press Truman during the Barkley-Harrison imbroglio was related to the president's unwillingness to speak for his friend. Farley had called Pendergast asking the boss to call Truman on the very day of the Colorado Springs summit meeting. It is also possible that Stark tipped off the Roosevelt administration as to the possibility of making the call on the same day that he was pushing the boss around.

Not long after the Colorado Springs meeting a fortuitous event played into the hands of Stark. What brought the Pendergast bribe out of the realm of rumor, which is where it was in 1935–1937, into the realm of fact, and allowed Stark to get action from the Roosevelt administration, was sheer happenstance. It stands revealed in a book Milligan published in 1948 in which he sought to connect the then president of the United States with the scandals of the Pendergast machine (Milligan thoughtfully published the book in the year when by all accounts Truman's presidency was going to be ended by Governor Thomas E. Dewey). Early in 1938, according to Milligan, a former Missourian, unnamed, decided to retire from the Bureau of Internal Revenue's headquarters in Washington, to remove to New York where he was taking another position. But before leaving the capital this official talked to a Washington reporter for the *Kansas City Star* and told him about Street's having received checks from fourteen large insurance companies totaling $100,500. He told the reporter that the bureau knew the checks had a connection with an important Missourian, not an officeholder, who in June 1936 was coming to New York on the maiden voyage of the *Queen Mary*, and that inspection of the passenger list showed the names of Mr. and Mrs. Pendergast. He related that Street later paid income tax on the checks.[30]

Why the retiring BIR official informed the reporter requires little imagination. The official leaked this information because nothing was happening to investigate Pendergast. The three-year statute of limitations on the bribery was running out that year, 1938. The sole case for the government would have to be income tax evasion. The best the bureau's agent in Chicago was doing was to pursue Street just short of the filing date for amending his 1935 return, March 15, 1937, and was then waiting to do the same for his 1936 return, which meant waiting until March 15, 1938. What also may have moved the retiring official, apart from his own retirement that made it safe to divulge information, was Street's death on February 1, 1938. The latter event meant that the procedure of waiting until March 15 had come to naught, since Street no longer was available for prosecution. As the head of the Treasury Department's intelligence unit later described what had happened, Street had fooled the bureau.

The *Kansas City Star* and Pendergast hated each other. The reporter telephoned Governor Stark in Jefferson City.

Stark descended on Washington and saw the president. One must believe that however inactive Roosevelt had seemed to Pendergast in 1937, inaction was better than the action that followed. Stark was in an excellent position to demand action from the president, and FDR would have found it impossible not to provide it. For one thing, it would have been clear that Stark was the coming man in Democratic politics in Missouri, and whatever services Pendergast had rendered in the past were no longer of account compared with those Stark could render in the future. For another, the president must have felt unable to withstand the pressure, for Stark could have leaked to the newspaper press what he knew about Pendergast, together with commentary that the Roosevelt administration had refused to stand up for right against wrong.

It is interesting that FDR had done nothing about Pendergast's huge bribe until forced to. The president was known privately not to be alarmed at wrongdoing, so long as it was not obvious and supported Democratic purposes. He had started his political career as a protégé of one of the Tammany bosses who later went to jail. When he moved against Mayor James J. Walker of New York in 1932, it was not until Walker's behavior became so outrageous that the then governor had to do something. He cooperated on numerous occasions with the Pendergast machine. Farley in 1931, surely with Roosevelt's knowledge, may have made the deal for the delegate votes. Roosevelt gave the machine patronage of all sorts. He displayed no concern about ghost votes in 1932 and 1936.

A native of Missouri, Ewing Y. Mitchell, worked hard for Roosevelt's nomination and election in 1932, became assistant secretary of commerce in the new administration, and found no spirit of reform in its ranks. The Commerce Department in 1934 published an account of itself, *United States Department of Commerce: How It Serves You on Land, and Sea, and in the Air*. That year the liner *Morro Castle* burned, and it became evident that the liner's captain had not held regular fire drills; the administration suspended his license for ten days. The next year a TWA plane ran out of gas while flying over Missouri, and the resultant crash killed, among others, Senator Bronson Cutting of New Mexico. Mitchell reported these delinquencies to his department's secretary, Daniel C. Roper, and that was the end of that. Meanwhile, in 1934, the assistant secretary had gone out to Missouri before the 1934 primary and appealed publicly for citizens to move against Pendergast. Protests went to Washington, and Mitchell sent evidence of fraud. The result was a move to obtain Mitchell's resignation, and the president relieved him on June 15, 1935.[31]

In 1937, the year before the Pendergast crisis arose, Farley went to the president outraged over discovery that an underling of Boss Frank Hague of Jersey City was opening the mail of one of Hague's political opponents. An honest man, if a political manager, Farley asked for the underling's prosecution, under an Act of Congress of 1878 that carried a penalty of up to two thousand dollars in fines and imprisonment of up to five years for opening or interfering with private letters. The president told the postmaster general that to go after Hague's lieutenant would not be a good idea. "Forget prosecution," he said. "You go tell Frank to knock it off. We can't have this kind of thing going on. But keep this quiet. We need Hague's support if we want New Jersey."[32]

The president's papers in the Franklin D. Roosevelt Library at Hyde Park, New York, do not supply any enlightenment on the question of whether in May 1936 or shortly thereafter, at the time of the *Queen Mary's* arrival, Roosevelt learned about Pendergast's bribery. The voluminous diaries and papers of Secretary of the Treasury Henry Morgenthau, Jr., also in the Roosevelt Library, have nothing to say about whether FDR's Hyde Park neighbor learned about Pendergast from the BIR and went to the president with the issue.[33]

After the notable retirement of the BIR official, matters in regard to Pendergast moved with a rapidity they altogether had lacked. President Roosevelt immediately went over to Stark, a fact that Farley discovered on March 22, 1938. A few days before, the postmaster general had talked with Truman, who told him he wanted to name his friend Fred Canfil, the deliverer of his speeches during the 1934 senatorial campaign, as federal marshal in Missouri. Farley said he would speak to the president. But on March 22, Roosevelt told Farley to talk to Stark about Canfil's appointment. The issue appeared three more times in Farley's diary, on March 30, April 9, and April 19, but to Farley's displeasure the president now felt that Stark needed to be consulted. The president told him on April 19 that Stark and Pendergast were going to have a battle for control. Farley told FDR that "I didn't think it fair that Stark have anything to say about this appointment because it is Federal." The president refused to make the appointment.

All the while an investigation of Pendergast was going forward. After talking with the president Stark called Milligan in Kansas City and asked him to come to Washington. The Treasury Department assembled its top officials, and Milligan long remembered the looks on their faces as they heard Governor Stark, who gave no expression one way or the other, tell them what was in their own files. The head of the treasury's intelligence unit, Elmer L. Irey, put his best man, Rudolph H. Hartmann, on the case. Hartmann had broken the Lindbergh case. He soon came on the telegram to the St. Louis bank, which was the providential lead after the providential retirement.[34] In June 1938 came a sure sign that discoveries were in course. The director of the Federal Bureau of Investigation, J. Edgar Hoover, gave a speech before a business organization in Nashville and discussed the "debauchery of law and order" in large cities. He singled out the "gory scenes of multiple crimes" and the "armed fury of entrenched interests" in Kansas City and related that "today the throne of the leader of this machine is toppling."[35]

And so by the summer of 1938 a federal inquiry into Pendergast's income tax payments, or lack of payments, was underway, with the support of President Roosevelt, and giving promise of turning up enough evidence to convict the boss and bring the collapse of the machine. To this had been added the investigation into the machine's voting excesses in the 1936 election. And in addition, early in 1939 came an attack by a Kansas City circuit judge, a Democrat from Independence, Allen C. Southern, on the city's gamblers and other criminal elements, owners and operators of what were known locally as "the joints," such night places as the Fortune Club and the Snooker Club. These places had made the city known as the Paris of the Plains. During a six-week period early in 1939, when his turn came up under a rotation system to exercise state criminal jurisdiction, Southern moved against the night people, bringing in 167 indictments against many machine politicians and their friends, who were heavily involved. The exact amount of money that was taken in by the city's well-known illegal clubs was a matter of dispute, a common estimate being that they did an annual gross of $12 million. Judge Southern believed it was $20 million. Where the machine was involved was in the lug placed upon profits to ensure protection by the local police. Milligan showed that annual collections on nineteen joints had gone from $53,161 in 1935 to $103,275 in 1938. The total number of illegal places was estimated in the dozens, as many as several hundred. It was estimated that Pendergast received 40 percent of the collection, with the rest divided among five or six others in the syndicate.[36]

In bringing the indictments Southern excluded the county prosecuting attorney, W. W. Graves, Jr., a machine official. Graves, he knew, would do his best to obfuscate the drawing up of indictments and subsequent prosecutions, making a mockery of what Southern was attempting. Graves filed suit over his exclusion, the case went to the Missouri Supreme Court, Southern traveled to Jefferson City to defend himself, and the court—having already proved its mettle by voting against the O'Malley insurance compromise—supported Graves's exclusion.

During the Southern investigation a federal case against the Kansas City criminal element was being developed by Judge Reeves, who impaneled another grand jury.

For the income tax case against Pendergast time was necessary to comb the Chicago records, and meanwhile Governor Stark shoved everyone in Washington, impatient to get Pendergast. Late in March of 1939 he went to the president, complaining that two Justice Department men, James W. Morris and Brien McMahon, were delaying matters. He was promised that Hartmann would testify to the new grand jury impaneled by Judge Reeves, which had taken up the Pendergast investigation. A treasury representative called the office of Attorney General Frank Murphy and told him how hard the governor was pushing. Undersecretary of the Treasury John W. Hanes held a meeting on March 29 and said that "Governor Stark called the Secretary up on the phone. . . . just worried the hell out of him." On his own, Hanes called Stark, and did not get very far:

> S: Hartmann—Hartmann will get a lot of information to close your case, undoubtedly, because this thing is breaking, you see.
> H: Yes.
> S: It would be suicidal to delay it for two reasons. The public opinion out here just wouldn't stand for it; we'd have a scandal; they'd all know about it, you see?
> H: Yes. Well now, Governor, I—I think you'll find everything in order.

S: Thank you, sir. . . . And if I can help you at any time I want to do it, sir.

H: Well, you are very kind and we appreciate it. I—I'm glad we got it fixed to your satisfaction, and I hope it goes all right, but I—I was anxious . . .

S: You keep your weather eye on it and see that there are no delays, will you please, sir?

H: Yes, sir.[37]

Treasury representatives desired to hold off on an indictment, for they were checking into Pendergast's companies and wanted to indict him for failure to pay income tax on profits from them, as well as on the insurance bribe. Representatives of the treasury pleaded with Murphy not to indict the Kansas City boss until they were ready, but Murphy saw an opportunity to take credit for everything and flatly refused to wait. (He does not seem to have had a telephone call from Governor Stark.) A sign appeared on April 4, 1939, when he and J. Edgar Hoover flew out to Kansas City. Governor Stark, with inside information, wrote Tuck Milligan the next day: "That brother of yours is doing a marvelous job and I am all keyed up waiting for the Federal Grand Jury to give us the big news. It will be a great day when it comes."[38]

The great day, anticipated by so many of the boss's enemies, required two days, a month and a half apart. On the day of indictment, April 7, the boss appeared in the U.S. marshal's office and affirmed his good faith and character and total lack of connection with the allegations that had come down from the grand jury. He was indicted on Good Friday, and when taking off his coat to be fingerprinted said to no one in particular, "There's nothing the matter with me. They persecuted Christ on Good Friday, and nailed him to the Cross."[39]

Then the past closed in on the present. Evidence against him was overwhelming. The government brought a second indictment showing that since 1927 he had juggled accounts of nine companies and used employees to receive stock dividends, salaries, or loans they paid back to him. His failure to pay taxes on business income amounted to much more than failure to pay tax on the insurance bribe. After the second indictment Pendergast's accountant promised cooperation with the grand jury and leaped, or was pushed, from a bridge, with account books and two suicide notes left in his abandoned automobile.

On May 22, 1939, Pendergast threw himself on the mercy of the court, pleading guilty to both indictments. This brought him face to face with Judge Reeves's colleague, Judge Otis, as dedicated a servant of the law as Reeves—born on a Missouri farm, devotee of the classics and the Bible, graduate of the law department of the University of Missouri, appointed to the federal bench in 1925 by President Calvin Coolidge.[40] He sentenced Pendergast to fifteen months in prison and fined him $10,000 on the first count, in addition to $350,000, and because of his poor health placed him on five years' probation on the second count.

O'Malley was served with a summons as he came out of a church in Baltimore; he was visiting his son in the East. He, Graves, and Matt Murray went to prison. Otto P. Higgins, director of the Kansas City police, the last person who talked to Pendergast's bookkeeper before his suicide, followed them. McElroy resigned, and shortly afterward eight treasury agents spread out across the city seeking the threads of his multifarious dealings. In addition to juggling the city's accounts he had juggled money to himself: the agents discovered his use of a real estate agent, H. H. Halvorson, as a funnel for money, and that between 1933 and 1938 the city manager had failed to report $274,263.15, upon which $62,326.27 was due. On September 14, 1939, subpoenas were issued for witnesses to appear before the grand jury on September 18. On September 15, McElroy died, of uremia and heart disease, having appealed his case, as the head of the treasury agents put it, to a higher court.[41]

The collapse of the machine was acutely embarrassing to Senator Truman. His first instinct was to defend his mentor, and a *Kansas City Star* reporter took his photograph in his office standing next to a signed picture of Pendergast. He told the reporter he would not desert a sinking ship. According to the *Star* the senator amended his remark about the destination of the ship; he said he did not wish to leave a ship in distress.

Truman was in a near impossible situation. Shortly before the debacle he took Jim Pendergast to see Farley. In his presence Jim asked Farley to intervene. Truman called Farley later and apologized.[42]

President Roosevelt pushed him again, unmercifully, just before Pendergast fell. After the president lost the fight over the Supreme Court he sought a law allowing him to reorganize the executive branch of the government by executive act, subject to congressional veto within sixty days. The proposed law had the sponsorship of the nation's leading political scientists. Basically the idea of reorganization was a good one. The timing, however, was deplorable. A reporter from the *St. Louis Globe-Democrat* who was close to Truman, and after World War II wrote a short biography of the former senator, described the situation graphically: "The new fight was widening and deepening the party rift of 1937; almost half of the Democrats were in open rebellion and Roosevelt's leadership, sunk to its lowest level, was drifting still lower."[43] Privately Truman and many other senators, given President Roosevelt's lackadaisical administrative methods, did not find the proposal important. What they saw was a presidential effort, following failure of court reorganization, to shove another such proposal down their throats. When the vote came up on reorganization the president faced the possibility of another tie vote, as over the Barkley-Harrison contest. The closeness might well have been arranged to humiliate the president; most tie votes in the Senate are not accidents but managed affairs. Whatever, the embattled president turned on Truman, who was in a weak position, and shoved him.

Truman was in Missouri when the presidential request came in March of 1939. He was speaking to the state legislature in Jefferson City on the theme of good government. After the senator's address there was a luncheon, at which members of the legislature were present. Governor Stark came for the luncheon, but did not talk to the senator. Afterward Truman received telephone calls from Farley and the president's press secretary, Stephen T. Early, asking him to return immediately to cast his vote. Farley and Early told Truman his vote was crucial.

The senator took a dangerous night flight through a snowstorm, and arrived to cast the deciding vote. He arrived also in a furious mood, believing the administration was showing no respect because it thought it did not need to do so. Many years later when Truman's private papers opened, an account of what happened was discovered. The senator after voting called Early and snapped at him: "Well, I'm here, at your request, and I damn near got killed getting here by plane in time to vote, as I did on another occasion. I don't think the bill amounts to a tinker's damn, and I expect to get kicked in the — just as I always have in the past in return for my services."

"Well, Senator," said Early, "what is it you want?"

"I don't want a — — thing," said Truman. "My vote is not for sale. I vote my convictions, just as I always have, but I think the President ought to have the decency and respect to treat me like the Senator from Missouri and not like a — — office boy, and you can tell him what I said. If he wants me to, I'll come down and tell him myself."

"All right, Senator," said Early, "I'll tell the President."[44]

Nor was this the end. The president responded by inviting Truman to the White House the next day, where there was a very uneasy conversation. As was his wont, Roosevelt showed friendship for the Missouri senator, and interspersed his concern and goodwill with the commentaries he intended to make. He thanked Truman for his contribution to the important bill that passed the Senate because of Truman's vote. But throughout the conversation he showed detailed knowledge of what was going on in Kansas City. He mentioned a visit to Washington of Police Director Higgins. He inquired after Pendergast's health, which Truman assured him was excellent. He bluntly stated that he intended to clean up Kansas City politics.

Not long afterward the federal attorney for western Missouri was in Washington attending the annual conference of U.S. district attorneys. While there Milligan called on President Roosevelt. After complimenting the attorney on the excellent work of his office FDR said, "I told Harry Truman the other day that he had better get away from that crowd out there." Milligan, to be sure, knew what crowd the president was referring to.[45] The president was telling a Truman enemy a point that, in better circumstances, he might have reserved for the senator.

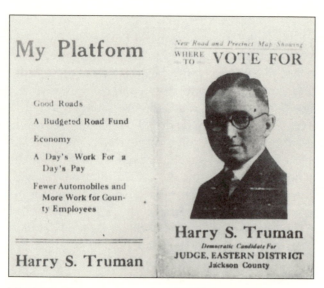

The 1922 campaign. Harry S. Truman Library.

Judge Truman and
Margaret, 1924.
Harry S. Truman
Library.

The Truman family, 1920s. Harry S. Truman Library.

A dinner for the senator-elect and his family, First Christian Church, Independence, December 17, 1934. Harry S. Truman Library.

In 1902, Thomas J. Pendergast was superintendent of streets in Kansas City, by appointment of Mayor James A. Reed, later U.S. senator.

Pendergast liked to have his picture taken in a hat. Harry S. Truman Library.

The Pendergasts in Paris, 1935. Wedow Collection, Western Historical
Manuscript Collection, Kansas City.

The Democratic National Convention, Philadelphia, 1936. Left to right: Senator Truman, Pendergast, James P. Aylward, unidentified, James A. Farley, unidentified. Harry S. Truman Library.

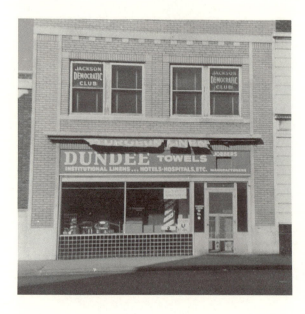

1908 Main Street, Pendergast's office. Wedow Collection, Western Historical Manuscript Collection, Kansas City.

The opening of the St. Louis National Horse Show Arena, September 27, 1937. Left to right: St. Louis Mayor Bernard L. Dickmann, Governor Lloyd C. Stark, Senator Bennett Champ Clark, Senator Truman. Witmer Collection, Western Historical Manuscript Collection, St. Louis.

NO PLACE FOR A KIDDIE CAR

MARCH 29, 1940

"No Place for a Kiddie Car," a Daniel R. Fitzpatrick cartoon in the *St. Louis Post-Dispatch*, March 29, 1940. State Historical Society of Missouri, Columbia.

A Stark Club of Chicago poster in July 1940 pushing Stark's candidacy for the vice-presidency. Western Historical Manuscript Collection, Columbia.

Downtown Sedalia, 1940, during Truman's campaign. Victor R. Messall papers.

In front of the courthouse at the Sedalia rally. Harry S. Truman Library.

The senator's eighty-year-old mother, Martha Ellen Truman, on the platform at Sedalia. Harry S. Truman Library.

Bess W. and Margaret Truman, 1940 primary. Bess once said that a wife's task during a campaign was to keep her mouth shut and her hat on straight. Harry S. Truman Library.

Introducing the senator in Sedalia. Harry S. Truman Library.

(From Truman State Campaign Headquarters, 313 S. Ohio, Sedalia, Mo.)

CAMPAIGNING FOR RENOMINATION MEANS WORK EVEN TO A UNITED STATES SENATOR

SEDALIA, MO.—United States Senator Harry S. Truman at his State Headquarters here, checking over campaign material with his manager, Victor R. Messall of Joplin. The Senator has been kept quite busy, with a campaign on his hands in Missouri and the national emergency, occasioned by the European crisis, occupying his attention in Washington. In addition to that, he is Missouri's representative on the important Platform Committee of the Democratic National Convention. "Work never hurt anybody," comments Senator Truman, one of the very few members of the Senate, regularly at his desk in the Senate Office Building in Washington before 6 A.M. daily.

A publicity release from the Truman campaign, 1940.
Victor R. Messall papers.

Campaign manager Victor R. Messall at the Sedalia headquarters. Harry S. Truman Library.

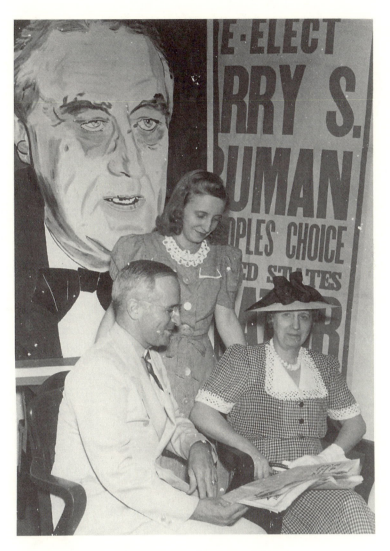

The senator and his family. Harry S. Truman Library.

Truman on the hustings
during the 1940 campaign.
Harry S. Truman Library.

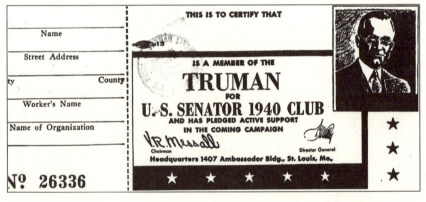

This card entitled members of the Truman for U.S. Senator Club to all the
club's privileges, which were none—apart from voting for the senator. Victor R.
Messall papers.

ONE MAN'S FAMILY---42 MEMBERS---ALL FOR TRUMAN

SEDALIA, MO.,—W. J. Cliffe of St. Louis, who recently completed 36 years as switch foreman with the Missouri Pacific, and members of his family, who are working for the renomination of United States Senator Harry S. Truman, according to Victor R. Messall of Joplin, campaign manager, with State Headquarters here. Besides Cliffe, the picture shows his four sons, their wives; seven daughters and their husbands; his 18 grandchildren and one great-granddaughter, who, although too young to vote, is doing her share in generating sentiment for Senator Truman among the kiddies of her neighborhood. Cliffe is standing near right-center. In sending the picture to Truman Headquarters here, a son, Raymond D. Cliffe, wrote "This congregation represents a 100 per cent. Truman support."

Truman supporters. Special Missouri issue of *Labor,* 1940. Victor R. Messall papers.

Jordan W. Chambers, St. Louis black political leader and a supporter of Truman. St. Louis Mercantile Library.

Truman and Mayor Dickmann, Jefferson Day Dinner, April 13, 1940. State Historical Society of Missouri, Columbia.

Robert E. Hannegan. Western Historical Manuscript Collection, St. Louis.

AFTER THE PRIMARIES TOMORROW

The *Kansas City Journal*, one of the few Missouri newspapers favoring Truman's renomination, predicts Governor Stark's defeat. Victor R. Messall papers.

3

Organizing and Campaigning

With assignment of Pendergast to Leavenworth, Senator Truman came to the lowest
point in his political career. What he was
looking at was the end of his participation in politics.
What had happened was not his fault, but he was
blamed for it. He was the gentleman from Pendergast,
the office boy, the bellhop, the one with calluses on
his ears.

Stark seemed unbeatable. At the time of Pendergast's downfall *Life* magazine arranged a big article and
raised the possibility of the governor's becoming president. The magazine likened him to Dewey, pursuer of
criminals in New York City, and sought to show that
as Dewey might be the Republican standard-bearer in
1940, Stark would be the sensible Democratic candidate. In 1939, one should add, President Roosevelt's
desire for a third term was not yet clear.

But to his enormous personal credit, instead of sur-
rendering to Stark, the senator fought him. For the

months that remained in 1939, after the machine collapsed, Truman could only wait things out and in the course of it measure his chances. Early the next year, 1940, he made his move by filing for renomination in the primary that would take place on August 6. Then he sought to organize, prepare, bring in such supporters as he could, create an organization or at least the facade of one. Afterward he would go out on the hustings, which meant speaking to local crowds on whatever occasions he and his assistants could manage. In the summer of 1940 he went into dozens of Missouri's 114 counties. Each had its courthouse, and he and his driver passed from one county seat to the next, talking if not before service clubs or in school gymnasiums then on the steps of the courthouses themselves, afterward shaking hands and giving interviews to local reporters.

1

Truman began the organization effort by attempting to see where he was, and what he faced.

Knowing more than the editors of *Life*, the senator assumed that Roosevelt would go for a third term and receive one. That raised a question as to whether the president would back Stark for the Senate or at least stay neutral.

Here it was immensely difficult to know. He had not seen much of Roosevelt, but everyone in Washington knew that the president liked to hold his cards. The man was secretive. Moreover, FDR was not straightforward. The senator could not understand how the president botched the issue of reorganizing the Supreme Court. Truman wrote his wife that the court was fossilized on an 1884 basis, as the president said, and Roosevelt's approach was wrong. "He should have just plainly . . . said let's give it more new blood by appointing two or three young men on it. That's what the issue is and that's all it will ever be. . . . The Court has become the bulwark of Hooverism and reaction. They're not immortal nor infallible, so why not do the job in a straightforward way."[1]

Roosevelt had dealt contemptuously with the junior senator from Missouri, and Truman could not forget that. There was the Barkley-Harrison humiliation, after which the president ignored Truman for months. Early in 1939 it was the reorganization bill. After the majority leader affair, while at Fort Riley in the summer of 1938 doing his service as a reserve artillery colonel, he was feeling little affection for the president, and so wrote his administrative assistant, Messall: "The Chief Executive doesn't care a darn about the junior senator from Missouri . . ."[2]

Late in June 1939, Governor and Mrs. Stark had luncheon with the president and Mrs. Roosevelt at Hyde Park. FDR was host to twenty-four governors, and the Starks were at his table.

The senator sought eagerly to get FDR's opinion of Stark, and the president obliged in a dissembling way, giving the impression that Stark bored him. Senator Herring talked to the president who said that he, Roosevelt, hoped Truman would be reelected and added that Stark was "an egotistical fool."[3] FDR told another friend that he would do something "to take the governor off my back." Early in August 1939, Truman saw Roosevelt about a congressional bill "and he insisted on talking Missouri politics and telling me what a funny governor we have. He didn't say phony, but that's what he meant. Actual quotation: 'I do not think your governor is a real liberal. . . . He has no sense of humor. . . . He has a large ego.' " Roosevelt invited Truman to ride on his train across Missouri, and said: "Be sure and get on that train, for you can rest assured your governor will *without* any invitation."[4]

Not long afterward, and unbeknownst to Truman, the governor and the president got together on November 9, 1939, and Stark recorded the exchange on small, square slips of paper. The wily Roosevelt took back any words of support he had offered Truman:

> Pr: . . . Tru friends say Roos for T. vs Stark for Sen. Pr. give him job & tell can't get elected.
> LCS: Want keep in race easiest beat. Wait after Pri.
> Pr: Tell short time before Pri he'll get job & he won't work so hard.[5]

The president desired Missouri's electoral votes and knew who could provide them.

By this time, lacking further presidential intimations of support, Truman made his own move. He was planning to attend a gridiron dinner in St. Louis "where I suppose they are expecting to give me the works."[6] He asked several dozen of his supporters to meet him at the Statler Hotel, January 27–30, 1940.

A banker from Webb City in southwest Missouri, Harry Easley, got there first and had breakfast with the senator on the twenty-seventh, and not long afterward the two of them learned what President Roosevelt and Stark were up to. They had just finished breakfast when the telephone rang and it was the White House—Steve Early who desired to speak with Truman. Truman refused to talk to him, and Messall took the message. Early told Vic that if Truman would withdraw from the Senate race and not file against Stark, the president would name him to the Interstate Commerce Commission, a lifetime appointment at a salary of fifteen thousand dollars rather than Truman's senatorial salary of ten thousand. Truman said to Messall, "Tell them to go to hell because I've made up my mind that I'm going to run for the Senate."[7]

The meeting followed—which was not so much a meeting as a passage of people through the senator's hotel suite. Easley remembered that they were all encouraging, and yet this seems to have been a trick of memory. According to Truman's friend John Snyder, with whom the senator usually attended summer camp, only two people advised him to run. Snyder said he so advised, but could not assist in a campaign because he was a federal employee, in charge of the Reconstruction Finance Corporation's branch in St. Louis. Truman asked several of the people who came if they would accept committee assignments, and to a man they refused, giving one excuse or another.

The *Post-Dispatch* received word from somewhere, probably Stark, that Truman was getting an offer of federal employment. The same day that Early called, the *Post-Dispatch* published an account of the ICC offer, with editorial embellishment: "Harry Truman, the erstwhile Ambassador in Washington of the defunct principality of Pendergastia, is back home appraising his chances of being reelected to the Senate. They are nil. He is a dead cock in the pit." At the end of the senator's St. Louis visit he was forced to deny that he was seeking an appointment to the National Labor Relations Board: "There is no Federal job that I want. . . . Any report that I am not going to run for the Senate is not true."

An indication of how discouraging the St. Louis meeting was appeared some weeks after the senator was in the state's eastern metropolis, in an exchange between Easley and Truman's World War army friend Roger T. Sermon, the perennial mayor of Independence. Doubtless Truman never learned how bleak his prospects seemed to his two friends. Sermon had been blunt at the time of the St. Louis meeting. "Harry," he said, "I don't think you can win, not merely my personal opinion but after inquiry around." The senator's response was, "Old Mr. Gloom, I'm going to file. I wouldn't have the guts to go home and face my people if I ran out."[8] Sermon later wrote Easley that Truman's friends needed to do something for him, beyond cheering him up:

> Several days ago I took it upon myself to write to Bennett Clark, requesting that he do something toward getting Senator Truman a federal place. Of course, as you know, Truman states that he has never been offered a place, and I think it high time that someone is doing something to see that he is made an offer. Perhaps if you will write to Bennett too it will be more effective than my writing, for in order to get the Senator and his friends out of a bad hole, I think that somebody should take it upon themselves to see that such an offer is made.

The banker must have been told not to say anything about the phone call from Early and what the senator told Messall to tell the president. But he was as pessimistic as Sermon when he replied. He said he had been

> trying to pull what strings I could along the lines suggested by yourself. It looks like that unless a concerted effort to accomplish this end is put forth immediately things are going to develop into a terrible mess. Harry called me from Washington on Saturday afternoon and wanted to know if I wouldn't permit him to announce that I was going to handle his campaign. From this I think you can see that I am really in a hole. Personally, I feel that Harry is ignoring the Jackson County situation and listening to a group of jobholders in St. Louis who are interested in their job, and, consequently say the things to him that he likes to hear. Personally, I am not built along these lines. The situation is serious.[9]

But over the many years Truman had exhibited a trait that could assist him in serious situations, and he called upon it now. This trait, this fundamental part of his character, was an ability to stand up to adversity. He went from St. Louis to Kansas City and there, in the Hotel President, did what he believed he had to do.

At the Hotel President his closest friend in the city, Tom Evans, the drugstore owner, was present, together with Messall and a young assistant from Washington, Kenneth Miller. Truman for a short time was hesitant, mulling over his situation, something he often did. Contrary to what people thought, he never made a decision until he had to; he could make what he described as a jump decision, a temporary decision, but he would wait as long as he could, until the last minute, thinking things over. Evans remembered that the group talked around the subject until the senator spoke up: "I've decided one thing. Vic, you and Ken go down and file at Jefferson City. Go down today, and be sure and be there and file, because there's one moral cinch, if I don't get anybody's vote, I'll get the boss's [Mrs. Truman's] and my own."

"I can get you two more, my wife's and mine," Evans said. "I don't think Vic is eligible to vote, so you'll only be assured of four. Ken can't vote because he lives in Washington where they don't allow them to vote."[10]

The Kansas City meeting was on Friday, February 2. Vic and Ken went down on the Missouri Pacific and on Saturday morning waited until the secretary of state was ready to close his office at noon for the weekend. A Truman supporter, Frank Erhart of Kansas City, was with them and long remembered the astonishment that spread over that official's face as he read the filing document.[11]

The senator's statement for release in the Sunday morning papers, February 4, was in part as follows, and bore the stamp of Harry Truman: "I have worked hard and talked little and then only when it was necessary, and I believe that the voters of Missouri will want me to continue to represent them in the Senate."[12]

The deed done, the first for the forthcoming campaign, Truman arranged the appearance of support, seemingly a great organization of his friends that covered the outstate between St. Louis and Kansas City. He announced a campaign committee, a chairman and eleven vice chairmen. The chairman was a Springfield lawyer, Sam Wear, an attractive attorney whose loaf would be cast up by the waters in 1945 when President Truman nominated him to be U.S. attorney for the western district of Missouri, replacing Milligan. Vice chairmen were Frank H. Lee of Joplin, a congressman in 1933–1935, elected at large and discarded when his Republican district had its first opportunity to vote against him, for whom Messall had been administrative assistant and hence could sign him up; Philip Welch, mayor of St. Joseph (population seventy-five thousand, the only city in the state other than the metropolises, too small to count for much); and John Farrington of Springfield, James R. Wade of Sullivan, D. C. Campbell of Maysville, and Dr. W. L. Brandon of Poplar Bluff. Brandon was a physician, an old Truman friend, but his support did not mean a great deal because Poplar Bluff was a small place and heavily Republican—the chairman of the Republican state committee, Grover Dalton, lived in Poplar Bluff. Other vice chairmen were Delmar Dail of Marceline, Philip Groves of Neosho, Sterling McCarty of Caruthersville, Mortimer Levy of Moberly, and Frank Monroe of Sedalia (with whom Truman stayed overnight when asked to run for the Senate in 1934).

The committee set up divisions, with Mrs. Henry Clay Chiles of Lexington heading the Women's Division; the former Mary Bostian was a classmate of the senator at Independence High School, in the class of 1901. C. L. Blanton, Sr., owner of the *Sikeston Standard,* one of the half dozen friendly newspapers in the state, headed the Publicity Committee. Tom Evans took over the Radio Division, as befitted his co-ownership of the Kansas City station, KCMO. Tom Van Sant, a banker from Fulton, was chairman of the misnamed Budget Committee, for money never was budgeted—there was never enough. Van Sant referred to himself as Mr. Average Voter and helped Truman by talking to him that way, for he was shrewd in guessing what outstate voters wanted. Roy W. Harper of Caruthersville headed the State Office Committee, a catch-all betokening an effort to raise money from officeholders.

Dr. William J. Thompkins, recorder of deeds for the District of Columbia "by presidential nomination," was named general chairman of the Negro Division. Truman had obtained the office for Thompkins, and it was a leading source of jobs in the federal government. Thompkins was president of the National Colored Democratic Association, and during the campaign traveled Missouri in the senator's behalf.

The senator's campaign headquarters boasted three offices. Fred Canfil, who had been Truman's speech-deliverer during the campaign in 1934, was put in charge of the Kansas City office. It was not much of a place, for the Jackson Democratic Club was still operating and would give Truman what votes it could, not many because of virtual abolition of ghost voting and local disgust with excesses of the machine; Aylward had been astonished by the machine's actions and was running a separate slate. Canfil's principal task was to find speaking engagements for the senator. That probably was enough for Fred, a big bull of a man whom people he came in contact with usually thought was strange or odd. A friend, Easley, said he had a "dog-like devotion" for Truman but could think of little else to say for him. An enemy described him as "a very articulate individual. I don't think he missed a chance to do a lot of talking when the occasion presented itself."[13]

State headquarters, which was a nominal description, was at 313 South Ohio in Sedalia. It was established in April 1940 when Truman installed there one of his four Senate secretaries, Catherine Bixler. In those days there was no law against using the office staff on personal tasks such as campaigns. State headquarters was in an old store building that had been unoccupied for more than a year.

Messall, whose title was "campaign manager," was in charge in Sedalia. A slight, long-faced man with yellow hair, who years before had come to Missouri from western Kansas with his mother, he was not entrusted with much. One explanation for his small part in the organization was that John Snyder disliked him. Another of Truman's campaign assistants disliked him because the assistant was "John Snyder's boy." At the end of the primary Truman came to believe he was taking money. Soon after the November election Messall left the senator to open a public relations office in Washington. And so he was "plowed under." Truman told Easley that "Now, we're going to have Vic to set up an outstate office and we'll have all our campaign literature and everything in Sedalia. Vic don't know anybody in St. Louis and he'll run that office there in Sedalia."[14] After the initial rally of the campaign, held in Sedalia, the Sedalia office lapsed into unimportance, with Messall and his assistant, Catherine, doing envelopes, sending out literature.

The third headquarters office was in St. Louis. Clarence Turley, present at the January meeting, gave the senator half a floor of the Ambassador Building for use as headquarters. It allowed more room than the other two locations. It housed a volunteer, the local lawyer David Berenstein, who took the title of director general. Just what he did for the campaign was not very clear. He was retiring president of the Zionist Organization of St. Louis, and may have raised a little money. He spoke well, although what speeches he made and what they produced was uncertain. He organized Truman for Senator clubs in St. Louis wards, or so he said; such a task would have been difficult, perhaps impossible, and in any event the result was unrecorded. With one exception, a good idea he had along the way, he contributed no more to the campaign than did Canfil in Kansas City and Messall in Sedalia. Truman believed that like Messall he took money, and after the campaign he too vanished from the senator's horizons.[15]

Surveying the Truman organization behind the facade, there was a near chaotic arrangement.

Nor was there enough money to make up for organizational delinquencies. Seeking some financial basis for the campaign, Truman upon return to Washington after the Missouri meetings discovered that Messall—it must have been Vic's responsibility—had failed to keep a record of people whom the senator assisted in problems that came up, problems he represented as senator. The list would have been a basis for asking for contributions.

Another shock was Truman's inability to find a chairman of the finance committee, which he resolved in a barely acceptable way. The chairman needed to have a title, and at last he went to a man he had met in the army in 1917, Harry H. Vaughan, and who like Snyder was a reserve colonel of field artillery and could be listed as Colonel Vaughan. Unfortunately, the colonel knew almost nothing about Missouri: at the time he was out of the state, in Illinois, selling loose-leaf book equipment. A surviving piece of stationery shows him employed by the Heinn Company of Milwaukee, "originators of the loose-leaf system of cataloging," and carried his name as "H. H. Vaughan, district manager." He was broke, and told Truman his bank balance was "about $3.25." Truman said that was all right, for people would like him.[16] Appointed, he proved likable.

Vaughan was the best person Truman could get. Pudgy, round-faced, he gave the impression of being disorganized, which he was. One Truman supporter described him as slap-happy, attempting forty things at once, and insinuated he did not finish many.[17] But during a campaign that did not possess an overload of confidence, he was a good man to have around; he had a joke, printable or not, for every occasion.

Collecting money in 1940 probably was easier than collecting it earlier in the midst of the Great Depression, but the economy was barely moving upward and money was scarce, not least for a losing cause. Vaughan measured his responsibilities years later and said, "This was a Woolworth campaign if you ever saw one."[18] Altogether, donations reached $20,750.78. The cost of soliciting the money was $2,862.91, fourteen cents on the dollar, an acceptable figure. But the money raised was not nearly sufficient, considering that Aylward in 1934, with assistance of Pendergast, raised $35,000. At the end of the Truman campaign in 1940 there was a deficit of $3,685.89. Truman's friends made post-campaign contributions and the senator assumed the remainder.

There was one large contribution, of one thousand dollars, and all others, with a few exceptions, were one hundred dollars or less, usually much less. The campaign's single big contribution came at the outset, and was not collected by Vaughan who operated from St. Louis, but by Snyder who happened to be in Washington talking things over with the senator. Snyder would become secretary of the treasury under President Truman, and see much money, but for the rest of his life he never forgot that thousand dollars. He had been visiting in the senator's suite, walked to the elevator and went down, and was going out when he ran into his old friend from St. Louis, Horace Deal, who attended the St. Louis meeting. Deal said, "John, what happened to you? You look like you've just been run through the wringer."

"Well," Snyder said, "that couldn't be a better description as to how I feel." He told Deal the financial problem, apparently relating that Messall had no list.

"It's pretty bad isn't it?" Deal offered.

"Well," Snyder said, "it is."

Deal ventured, "Well, maybe it's not all that bad." Walking over to the fender of an automobile, he brought out his checkbook, wrote out a check, and gave it to Snyder. It was for one thousand dollars.

Snyder turned and rushed back toward the Senate Office Building, and upon opening the door said, "Come on, go up with me." Deal said he had been about to go up but now would not do so, and would go back to his hotel, and "if you need me, call me." Snyder ran back up, waving the check in front of Senator Truman.[19]

A story arose that the New York financier Bernard M. Baruch, accustomed to doling money for worthy political causes that supported his reputation as "adviser to presidents," gave money at the behest of Senator James F. Byrnes of South Carolina. Baruch had been born in South Carolina, and owned a huge estate there. Byrnes and Baruch were close, and the story had it that Baruch made contributions to the Truman campaign totaling four thousand dollars. Truman never spoke about them, and surely would have, if Baruch had made them, even though during his presidency he came to dislike the financier, who gave some advice and received an appointment as spokesman at the United Nations for what Baruch thoughtfully described as the Baruch Plan for limiting nuclear weapons with the Soviet Union. Baruch refused to support Truman's campaign in 1948, and the president had words with him. Later history aside, there has never been any evidence of a 1940 contribution, not to mention several.[20]

Truman's friends gave, such as N. T. Veatch, Jr., a Republican engineer; he was part of Judge Truman's two-man commission to supervise road building. His county engineer, Alex F. Sachs, like Veatch, gave one hundred dollars. The vice chairmen of the campaign committee gave similarly. Division directors gave as well. So did Berenstein. Roger Sermon, who owned a grocery store, gave $93.50. Railroads were important in Missouri, and Truman was working on the transportation bill, and the Brotherhood of Railway Signalmen gave one hundred dollars, the Order of Railroad Conductors one hundred and fifty, the Railroad Steamship Clerks five hundred.

Tom Evans saw to it that his drugstore suppliers came through, such as Harry Cooper, a competitor of Gillette in razor blades, who gave two hundred and fifty dollars. Al Manlin carried all of Tom's insurance and sent a contribution. So did Al Gasen, a drugstore operator in St. Louis. Also a St. Louis broker that helped finance Tom's chain, the Crown Drug Company. Evans himself was a prime target of Vaughan, who spared no words, although Tom was too shrewd for that. Vaughan sent a telegram on May 29 asking an advance of one thousand dollars "to be repaid as soon as funds are raised through sources already ensured." He followed with a letter: "as money begins to roll into our Treasury, we shall earmark it for repayment to the 'inner circle friends' who, realizing our need, have come to our rescue. Being now assured of our ability to repay the amount advanced—surely no later than sometime in August—we are confident that you will not fail me."[21] In an audit of the Truman campaign fund, loans from Evans and a businessman in Springfield, Lester E. Cox, totaled $1,750.[22]

The finance committee went to federal government offices in Missouri—the Reconstruction Finance Corporation, Internal Revenue Bureau, and Federal Housing Administration—hoping that some officers had obtained their jobs through the senator. But it was necessary to be careful because of the Hatch Act prohibiting participation in politics by federal employees. Messall advised Easley that relatives and friends were not prohibited.

A very special portion of federal employees in Missouri was, of course, the WPA, and here Truman and Stark vied for control, with the governor winning. There was a good deal of evidence that Stark "put the lug" on state employees, and Truman could do little about that, other than publicizing cases. Putting the lug, taking percentages from political employees, was standard procedure in states around the country, a large part of the cement that held county and state politics together. In the matter of federal employees, in particular the WPA, a lug was up to their state administrator. Matt Murray was in Pendergast's pocket until the early summer of 1939. His replacement was the superintendent of the Missouri state police, B. Marvin Casteel, who had the title of colonel. He was appointed not by the two senators, Truman and Clark, but by President Roosevelt, after consulting with Stark.

Senator Truman found he could get nowhere with the WPA. By that he meant soliciting support of the hundreds of foremen, time-keepers, and other nonrelief personnel. It was illegal to approach workers on the job. For his inability to get to the nonrelief people he blamed Casteel. His friend Easley, who had been Murray's deputy for two years and knew how the organization worked, and was close to the issue in southwestern Missouri, corresponded with Truman on the subject and both of them went after the colonel. Casteel was a slippery character and apparently was not merely refusing solicitation of his supervisory personnel but firing anyone who seemed a Truman supporter. As early as July 1939, Easley wrote Truman that "the Stark faction" was preparing to clean house. In September, outraged, he sent a telegram to his successor as deputy administrator in Jefferson City: "Protest indiscriminate discharge of our friends this morning." In early January 1940, the senator had a talk with the colonel, who assured Truman that "his whole ambition in life is to do the job as it should be and did not in any way want to jeopardize my interests." The situation improved for a short time, then went down.

On February 21, Truman wrote, "You told me when you left here that you wanted to set this thing up so it would not be unfavorable to me, and the policy you have been following has been just exactly the opposite and I don't like it." Casteel did not reply to this letter nor several others. What neither Truman nor Easley knew was that on April 6, President Roosevelt sent a handwritten note to an aide: "Tell Col. Casteel to go ahead and clean house of old Pendergast crowd. Not use W.P.A. against Gov. Stark in either [state Democratic] convention or Aug. primary." Casteel evidently went into action. A Truman supporter from McDonald County, W. G. Tracy, wrote the senator on June 25 to relate that "this time not a friend of Senator Harry Truman on the job, in a nonrelief position or a relief position. This makes it very hard for your friends to do anything for you."[23]

With such discouragement there was great difficulty raising money. Vaughan began a venture to "give or get ten dollars." Truman supporters received booklets containing membership cards in a Truman for Senator organization. Recipients presumably would find it less embarrassing to give, that is, themselves send back ten dollars, rather than get ten memberships. An accompanying brochure carried the more open inquiry, "Can you advance us some cash immediately? Please do."[24]

As the campaign wore down to primary day, funds in the several headquarters offices sank to new lows. Canfil typically did not report, but Messall in Sedalia was down to $53.16 on August 3, with three days to go before the primary. Vaughan's account stood at $69.84 on July 25; he did not testify for three weeks, but on August 15 revealed he had $5.96.[25]

In the last desperate days Vaughan took two or three hundred dollars from somewhere and converted it into one-and-one-half-cent stamps, to carry an unsealed communication, a letter, to perhaps twenty thousand voters in the St. Louis area, saying the campaign committee was out of funds and would appreciate one-dollar contributions. " . . . we are in need of $5000," the colonel testified, "which Senator Truman is in no position to furnish. We must go to his friends, and we are appealing to your sense of generosity to help us. All we ask is $1 from you." In a postscript he apologized, "Please excuse this 1½¢ postage. Our funds are limited. Our campaign is conducted on a very conservative and economical basis." The plea to twenty thousand voters brought in eight hundred dollars.[26]

The well-financed campaign of Governor Stark rolled along; although the figure seems unlikely, Stark reportedly collected five times as much as Truman. The governor charged the senator with having campaigned from a "slush fund" provided by Pendergast, about which no one, especially Vaughan, had the slightest idea. Truman's people were beside themselves over how to answer. They could not afford radio time, apart from free time on KCMO. They took refuge in a press release, of little value because in all Missouri only two daily newspapers, the *Kansas City Journal* and the *Jefferson City Daily Capitol News*, supported the senator.

2

Pendergast was the unspoken presence in the Truman campaign, and could not be mentioned, this when the senator was organizing the campaign and then opened it officially on June 15, 1940, with a rally at Sedalia. By this time the former boss was out of Leavenworth, back at Ward Parkway, his sentence reduced to a year and a day because of good behavior. As a prisoner he had been quiet and cooperative and when physically able—he suffered another coronary just after arrival at the prison because the merciless U.S. attorney general, Murphy, released his prison photograph to newspapers—took down dictation from prison physicians about prisoners' examinations and wrote up the reports. The old man had aged markedly and was feeble after his return to Kansas City. He was lonely in his big house, his wife having abandoned him, the reason being, it was said, that he had not told her about his racetrack debts. He was forbidden by court order to take part in politics for five years and could not go to his Main Street office. He occupied himself in an office at the cement company.

All the while, during the campaigning, Truman could be sure he was going to hear about Pendergast from the governor, who would miss no opportunity to talk about the Pendergast senator. Stark must have written his own speeches, for they bore his stolid stamp. He never missed an opportunity, in opening his campaign and following up, to flay Truman as the boss's man, ready to turn Missouri back to the reign of terror that the boss and his minions had created.

To try to discuss the Pendergast phenomenon was too difficult to attempt. To set it out would have required going into such complexities that the explanation could not have been convincing. Truman had walked an honorable course, straight and narrow, and yet could not really describe it without opening himself to more attacks from the governor.

The senator's best course, the one he chose, was to present himself as the simple, unadorned, common Missourian he was, and hope that if people heard him or read his speeches they would realize that he could not have been the cat's paw, the lackey, and all the other lurid names Stark bestowed upon him.

And so he turned to the campaign. Bulletin No. 1 of the campaign committee, which announced the Sedalia meeting, sought to take higher ground. If exaggeration, it at least must have been comforting to the senator after hearing about himself and Pendergast from the governor. The bulletin drew Truman as a statesman of major proportions. "His character is written into his record and his record is engraved in his character," announced the writer of this four-page mimeographed extravaganza, undoubtedly his Sedalia headquarters representative, Messall. How the character and record became mixed this way was difficult to imagine, but so the writer allowed. The bulletin enlarged upon its subject, with an ungrammatical twist: "His name is enrolled among the great men of the Earth and the greatest servant of his people."[27]

Twenty-five thousand announcements of the rally went out to Truman's friends, on stationery that looked as if it arrived from Western Union and contained the company's name at the top. Messall said that Senator Truman was "anxious to meet you personally Saturday June 15, 7:30 P.M. Court House, Sedalia, Missouri. This marks official Missouri opening 'Truman for Senator' Campaign." Vic listed subordinate attractions of the "magnificent demonstration, seldom witnissed [sic] in Missouri": a galaxy of out-of-town orators to eulogize the senator, three orchestras to engender enthusiasm, a score of entertainers. He promised refreshments.

The announcements instructed the senator's friends on how to make themselves known as they flocked into Sedalia. They were to decorate their cars with American flags, red and white streamers, and signs with such phrases as "Make Government Human with Men like Truman," "Boone County Trumanized," "Keep a True Man on the job—Senator Harry S. Truman," "Tried and True, That's Truman," "Senator Truman loyal to his Country, loyal to the people," "Safe with Truman." Passing through towns, automobiles were to honk their horns "until the crowd is attracted."

The rally was at the courthouse, which allowed seating outside on the grass for twenty-five hundred people. The day and evening, Saturday, 7:30 P.M., was well chosen, for it was a time when one always could raise a crowd; in those now forgotten years in small towns, farmers came in and joined townspeople in shopping and visiting on Saturday nights. Loudspeakers carried speeches to the four streets surrounding the courthouse block, which itself was in the exact center of the business district. Estimates of attendance varied, with the *Post-Dispatch*'s the lowest: four thousand people, which the paper maliciously remarked was fewer than Governor Stark attracted at his rally in Mexico, Missouri, a month earlier.[28] Attendance, one may conclude, was about equal. The speaking program began when Mayor Julian H. Bagby introduced the state chairman of the Truman campaign, Sam Wear. The mayor, who ought to have known, pronounced the rally the largest political gathering ever held in Pettis County.[29]

The senator's address was summarized in advance by Bulletin No. 1 as a historic document to be remembered by the generations of today and tomorrow. What Truman said has mostly been forgotten, but he did speak on one topic that proved historic a few years later in 1947–1948, when President Truman came out for civil rights. That afternoon in Sedalia he had dedicated the Colored Hospital. For his remarks in the afternoon and evening he solicited the help of Dr. Thompkins, and what he said that evening was so precise that one can see who wrote it:

> During the World War the need of men for an Army and for war industries brought more and more of the Negroes from rural areas to the cities. In the years past, lynching and violence, lack of schools, and countless other daily unfair conditions, hastened the progress of the Negro from the country to the city. In these centers the Negroes have never had much choice in regard to work or anything else. By and large, they work mainly as unskilled laborers and domestic servants. They have been forced to live in segregated slums, neglected by the authorities. Negroes have been preyed upon by all types of exploiters, from

the installment salesman of cloth, pianos, and furniture to the
vendors of vice. The majority of our Negro people find cold
comfort in shanties and tenements. Surely, as freemen, they are
entitled to something better than this.

There was more: "I believe in the brotherhood of man, not merely
the brotherhood of white men, but the brotherhood of all men before law."

It was an extraordinary thing to say in outstate Missouri, where
southern ideas and ways dominated. He probably read his text with
little oratory, no flourishes (his way with speeches), but the words
were some of the most eloquent ever heard in Missouri and even in
the nation. He was making a bid for black support in a tight race.
He remarked that the social life of Missouri blacks "will, naturally,
remain their own," his outlook then and later. But his words were
something to remember.

The great day and evening passed, and his three headquarters
turned to the publicity that sometimes moves campaigns and in
any event is inseparable from them. Here it was necessary to create
the impression that Truman was winning. Messall's press releases
related the campaign's astonishing momentum, a great swing to
the senator. Friends were at work in every part of the state. Messall
claimed to have established a dozen subheadquarters, although he
did not list them and their workers. He related a veritable cascade of
support from all parts of the state, such support that renomination
would be by the largest majority ever rolled up for a candidate in a
statewide vote in Missouri, although he did not go into particulars.

A press release of July 10 brought up the awkward subject of
whether President Roosevelt was for Truman or Stark, and quoted
the senator: "I rather think the voters of Missouri will decide who
will be the next Senator, not the President." The issue came out
into the open because Truman in April declared that the president
had "expressed the hope that I would come back to the Senate next
year." FDR in fact had done this, in one of his dust-raising talks with
the senator and his supporters. Stark made an issue of Truman's
statement: "I know, of course, that this was ridiculous and untrue."
Man of action that the governor was, he forced the president into a
corner, knowing that when the president got into a corner he might
lie his way out, which is what happened:

history. And this age has come upon us so rapidly, that we haven't been able to adjust ourselves to it, and that's the cause of most of our troubles. That's the cause of unemployment . . ."[34] The explanation was none too helpful, for it begged the point, but was as good as any.

Another speech, essential in rural Missouri, was about the plight of farmers during the Depression. Farmers made the nation what it was. No nation, even if mercantile or industrial, emancipated itself from the soil. "Man has not reached the point where he can live abundantly and virtuously in stone and macadam, clustered around elevator shafts, in the midst of a synthetic flora and fauna created by the captains of industry." He spoke at New Franklin on June 27 about what farmers had done for America. The country's development had been naught but an extension of rural life. Cities were based on wealth from the farm: "Left to itself the city would soon collapse." History proved this point time and time again.[35] At St. Louis on July 31, though his audience was hardly farmers, he told them the truth, that the great Mississippi Valley was the richest place on earth for things to eat and wear. In all history it had no equal: "The Nile in its plenteous days could never hold a candle to the Mississippi Valley." The farmers' plight needed improvement, but it was a marked improvement over what prevailed at the beginning of the Roosevelt administration. In 1933 farmers' income was $4.6 billion. In 1939 it was $8.2 billion and with agricultural payments from the federal government $9 billion. The increase, if not ideal, showed that "if there's any farmer in this Mississippi Valley who has little enough sense to vote the Republican ticket this fall, he ought to have his head examined."

A third speech, designed to make sense in the isolationist Midwest in 1940, was about national defense. That summer a national issue was the draft bill, the first in peacetime, which the Roosevelt administration was pushing through Congress, with barely enough votes to pass. Here Truman took a position according to his lifelong belief that the country needed all young men in the National Guard or something similar. During the World War he had hated West Pointers, and when he became president would have been ready, if the country had gone along, to close West Point and Annapolis, or denominate them senior war colleges, relying on universal military training. At the Women's Jefferson Democratic Club of Saline County in Marshall on June 26, he announced that "the backbone of any

I called the White House to determine what I could say to the public about this matter. The White House reported back to me, after conferring with the President, that the President said there was absolutely nothing to this and that the President is taking no part in the senatorial race in Missouri. The White House has authorized me to make public this information in answer to this erroneous and unfounded rumor.[30]

This prompted Truman to tell Missouri voters to make up their own minds. He reminded them of the president's effort in 1938 to "purge" senators in Maryland, South Carolina, and Georgia, an effort that failed. He reminded them that the president had been very friendly, that he, Truman, never had asked him personally whom he favored. He said Senator Barkley (he may have meant Herring) had interviewed the president, who told him he would like to see Truman return to the Senate.

Messall's press releases did some good, but Truman's representative in Sedalia scored a triumph by arranging the printing of half a million copies of a special four-page Missouri edition of the railroad brotherhoods' weekly newspaper *Labor*.[31] The printing was enough to get the senator's campaign message, what he was attempting to do, into the hands of nearly every voter in Missouri. It came out in July, just before the primary, and told everything possible about the senator. The front page carried photographs of Truman and his mother, with his mother listening to "her boy's speech" at Sedalia. The righthand story related that the senator barred mudslinging in his campaign—meaning in part that he would not talk about Pendergast. Explanatory lines at the top of the first page related, among other things, that he had won the confidence of "F.D." Below were testimonies by Senators Barkley, Robert F. Wagner of New York, and Byrnes. In a box on the front page were his comments about race relations offered at Sedalia: "I believe in the brotherhood of man . . ." Another box related a tribute by the chaplain of the American Legion in Missouri, the Reverend Father M. F. Wogan. On inside pages were photographs of the two Truman women. A cartoon pointed out that Truman's record for labor was perfect. Moreover he was concerned for farmers. He had declared that if you hurt the farm you ruined the factory. The back page showed a cartoon of a worker and a farmer putting up the keystone to the arch of partnership. This page reiterated Truman's racial views: "Truman Demands Fair Deal under Law for Negroes." On that page, among other items, was the interesting comment, perhaps directed at F.D., that Truman was no "yes man."

The railroad brotherhoods had fifty thousand members in Missouri and their members would speak to other union members and their families. Bulletin No. 1 had announced that "Senator Truman Starts Out With a Solid Labor Group of 200,000 Strong and With an Assured General Support of an Additional 165,000 From Other Sources." The brotherhoods were leading the way.

Truman indeed did look good to railroad workers and other laboring people. The Wheeler-Truman Transportation Bill had occasioned hearings that showed Truman against the bankers and lawyers who had taken over the nation's bankrupt railroads. He helped publicize the plight of railroad laboring men, whose numbers went down dramatically in the 1930s; in 1926 the roads employed 1.7 million men with a payroll of $2.9 billion, and by 1936 employment was down to half, 860,000 with $1.7 billion in wages. Railroads blamed the government for a wage increase in 1936, higher taxes, and generally not appreciating their problems. Truman endeared himself to railroad labor in 1938 when the roads sought to cut wages by 15 percent; in testimony before a fact-finding board he concluded that banker management should not be permitted to sacrifice railroad labor.

But the most important part of the campaign, once on its way, was the senator's speeches. Here the press releases gave the barest indication of what he was up to.[32] A release of June 25 did inform supporters and all those who were about to be supporters that the senator had arrived at his executive campaign committee headquarters, meaning St. Louis, the day before. He would visit state campaign headquarters at Sedalia on Wednesday, June 26, on Thursday would attend a bridge dedication at Miami, and that evening would speak to the Howard County Young Democratic Club at New Franklin. Friday and Saturday, June 28 and 29, he would tour central Missouri, then leave for Washington on Saturday night. After attention to his senatorial duties he would fly back to speak at Marceline and Kirksville on Wednesday, July 4, and at Columbia on Saturday night, July 6.

He was to be back at his desk in Washington the following Monday, July 8. But he wrote his wife on July 7 that the week beginning

Monday, July 8, he would be at Van Buren, Willow Springs, Thaye West Plains, Mountain Grove, Cabool, Houston, Salem, Rolla, Stee ville, Sullivan, Washington, Jefferson City, Fulton, Mexico, Moberl and Hannibal.

Sunday, July 14, through Wednesday, July 17, he would be Chicago as a delegate-at-large to the Democratic National Conve tion "as Missouri's representative on the important Platform Co mittee." Thursday through Sunday, July 18–21, he visited ten m Missouri places. Monday through Wednesday, July 22–24, he was the nation's capital, "and start out again," as he wrote Bess. Thursd through Sunday, July 25–28, nine more places. After a Sunday re Monday and Tuesday, July 29–30, he spoke in seven places, w St. Louis on Wednesday the thirty-first.

Truman had a framework for his speeches: don't engage in pers alities and avoid mentioning opponents in any way; avoid controv sial issues and run on the record; don't get into issues unconnec with the primary; try to make the press see the light but unde circumstances attack the press; work for the party. Pendergast not in the framework.

For the most part Truman wrote his own speeches this t Snyder remembered that Berenstein and "a Mr. Goodman," the l a literary man, were helpful. But for the rest of it Truman pu speeches together; they had the ring of the senator, with turns flourishes. Actually there was no one else who could have done t Vaughan could not have written any; the colonel was no literary Nor was Messall. An assistant in Truman's senatorial office, Edg Faris, remembered that "Victor couldn't write a speech." Faris him as a shrewd, smart operator, who obtained knowledge observation, but lacked depth and was not much educate might have graduated from high school but Faris was uncerta

The speeches were only locally reported, and the senator repeat them, and Snyder recalled several that he used accord audiences. One concerned the Great Depression, still in evi A press release of July 13 when he was at Moberly and Ha announced him as saying that "wild greed" brought the Depr He meant the greed of bankers and lawyers, the same peop brought down the railroads. He admitted what everyone said the Depression, that it had been such a perplexing experie St. Louis on July 31, he said, "We're living in the greatest

Democracy is a well trained citizen army on the Swiss plan." At his speech in St. Louis he faced up to the draft bill: "Now, I don't believe in conscription; I do believe in a universal service to the country that you love . . . There isn't a kid in this United States who can't almost automatically drive a tractor and we have the brightest young men on earth. We ought to train enough of these young men . . ."

At St. Louis he went into detail not merely about farmers but about the country's foreign policy during the 1920s and 1930s, the policy that had brought on the administration's request for conscription. His account was approximately correct. He said that for years he and his colleagues in the Senate had been asking for a plan of national preparedness, but every time they asked, "the fellows who had outlawed war would cry us down and call us all war mongers." He was referring to the Kellogg-Briand Pact of 1928 outlawing war and to the peace movement that had helped produce the antiwar treaty and supported the neutrality acts of the 1930s. In the Senate he and his friends sought a "plain, common-sense national defense setup to defend the Monroe Doctrine." He said that the American people did not wish to attack anyone, did not desire more land, did not wish to take anything from anyone, were not angry with anyone in the world. Neither were people in the Netherlands, Norway, and Belgium, and "look where they are now." The fault lay, he did not say it openly, with Republican administrations, which had sponsored not merely the Kellogg-Briand Pact but the naval disarmament conferences. "We took the greatest navy in the world out into the Atlantic Ocean, and sank it—sank a lot of battleships and cruisers and gunboats." (This last was a bit of exaggeration. The U.S. Navy in the 1920s had not been the greatest navy in the world—that was the British Navy. The conferences abandoned a naval building program that had hardly started, and two battle cruiser hulls were converted into the later very useful aircraft carriers *Saratoga* and *Lexington*. The navy's cruisers were old and hence scrapped. As for gunboats, no fleet of importance used gunboats.)

Such was the oratory, and there remains some account of how Senator Truman went from place to place and spread the messages of his candidacy. This after his headquarters people managed meetings. It then was up to the senator and his driver, Fred Whittaker, and if an outdoor speech the operator of his sound truck, John A. Earp. Sometimes the group numbered four, counting Vernia Earp.[36]

The sound truck usually arrived ahead of the senator, to publicize the meeting. Earp would be there an hour early and would drive around to get up a crowd. Beyond announcing the place and time, Earp played band music, and that could cause problems. He remembered an experience of his partner who handled the sound for Truman's 1934 campaign. The partner had driven through some southern town in Missouri playing "Marching through Georgia"; Truman was in the vicinity and came running out, waving his arms, shouting "Get that — thing off. They'll kill me down here." In 1940 there was a different problem at Hannibal where a local judge, supposedly a loyal friend and booster, assured Earp that everything was arranged, turn on the sound. Most larger towns had ordinances prohibiting sound on the streets. The ordinances usually meant nothing and it was all right. After talking to the friendly judge a sixth sense held Earp back. Fred Canfil, on the scene, urged him to begin, but Earp decided to wait for the senator. He checked with the police department and discovered that the judge had put out an order that as soon as Earp opened up the police were to arrest him. He did not see Truman until after the meeting that night, when the senator came up and shook his hand, thanking him for being alert. Truman said it saved embarrassment. "Later that night, after a dinner meeting," Earp remembered, "Harry was in a rage—the only time I ever saw him turn purple."

It was several weeks of long, hard days for the senator and his driver and Earp, who started at sunup and ended each day about midnight. They traveled three or four hundred miles daily, with as many as eight stops. Truman gave the same speeches. Because he had setpiece talks he memorized them, bringing in a little local color. "I have never known a man that knew as much about the politics of Missouri as Mr. Truman did," Earp recalled. "He knew every little detail."

The Earps long remembered the later president of the United States. One point Truman made on many occasions, remarking it in speeches but also in conversation. He said he never met a man he couldn't learn something from. After one speech he came up to Vernia Earp and asked, "Mrs. Earp, how did you think the people reacted to my speech? Do you think they were for me or against me?" She said, "for," to be sure. According to her husband the senator "constantly asked the crew traveling with him if there was anything he could do to improve himself, if he was doing anything wrong." Earp said, "We were frank in telling him and he did gain a little polish." On one occasion Canfil had the nerve to say, "Yes, for God's sake, Harry, quit using that word asinine." The group agreed it was not a good word. Truman had a habit of slapping his hands together, in emphasis. During one of the group sessions Earp told him not to do that, as it caused the speaker cones to jump right out and seize the audience. Local people coming up to the rostrum to introduce the senator often blew sharply into the microphone to see if the sound was on, forcing Earp to retard the gain. He mentioned this to Truman who thereafter told them the equipment was on, to start talking in a normal voice.

Vernia Earp fondly remembered the many speeches: "I thought he was a wonderful speaker." Her husband was more restrained: "Well he was effective. He wasn't what you might call a good orator by any means, but he was effective." The senator spoke positively, did not criticize—as he told Snyder he would refrain from doing; at no time did Earp hear a derogatory remark. His speeches were concise, brief. "He had a message; he didn't pull any punches. He delivered it and it was short. He always cited an old Baptist minister he knew that said no soul was ever saved after twenty minutes." Earp knew the timing and could walk off, buy a Coke or something, come back nineteen minutes later, and wind things up.

The Earps were on the senator's side, and one time became so enthusiastic the senator thought them "carried away." Truman had complimented the sound man on the way he handled the equipment, and Earp said that the next time the sound truck went on the road the signs would read, "Truman for president." The senator scoffed at the idea.

4

Victory

In the Senate primary campaign in Missouri in 1940, just to hear the oratory of Stark made everything seem simple.

> What does it mean to the people of Kansas City if the machine succeeds in putting its senator back in power? For when the Pendergast gang marches its minions to the polls on August 6 to put the Pendergast senator back in power—when all the enemies of clean and honest government rally their forces—for the supreme effort to regain a death-grip on our state—they will be striking at the very liberties which you so recently tore from their clutches.[1]

But it was a complicated politique that brought the Senate contestants together, and despite the governor's speeches the contest was hardly a matter of light versus darkness. Truman had done his best for good government and was in a desperate fight for survival. The organization of his campaign was haphazard, to put the case at its best; his offices in Kansas City, Sedalia, and St. Louis were badly directed by a grab bag of the senator's supporters. He spoke from dawn to dusk and beyond, and spoke well, and probably managed to do little more than counteract the incompetence of his Hydra-headed headquarters.

The senator would not have won if it had not been for several developments. One was the coming of members of the Senate to his support, and notably the movement into Truman's camp of the state's senior senator, Bennett Clark. A second was the campaigning of Stark and Milligan. Both lacked charisma, to use the later word; they could not make themselves attractive, and with only a little encouragement, sometimes from opponents, they did the opposite. In the case of Milligan, his very entrance into the campaign assisted Truman in a special way. And lastly there was a crucial trade-off of votes by Democrats in a few counties of the small Bootheel of the state, in the remote southeast, the vicinity of the towns of Caruthersville and New Madrid. These Democrats had gathered under the leadership of the remarkable local politicians who understood how in combination their votes gave them power to elect statewide candidates, and worked out a deal to support the St. Louis candidate for the governorship, Lawrence McDaniel, in exchange for which the St. Louis machine wards would vote for the Bootheel's senatorial candidate, Truman.

1

Within a bare six years the junior senator from Missouri had managed to achieve stature in the upper house, and this fact gave Truman strength against his opponent Governor Stark. It gave him more strength than Stark calculated. The Senate, as Stark should have known, is a proud place; its members feel themselves anointed for their work of serving the nation and, alas, sometimes themselves. But whatever their occasional confusion of purposes, the members of the august upper house will unite against all outsiders, and this happened in Truman's case. It was not difficult for Truman's fellow senators to feel that President Roosevelt by siding with Governor Stark was interfering in the Senate's prerogatives. After the failure of his Supreme Court initiative the president in 1938 tried the purge and it failed. The situation in Missouri gave evidence of a similar purpose, for the president was attempting to elect his own man despite Truman's excellent record.

Stark walked into this situation. The governor of course gave the impression he was Roosevelt's representative. All Democrats across the country did that. The New Deal was popular and they tried to get as much support as they could from associating themselves with it. But there was a fine line, beyond which attempting to gain support could seem to be subservience and a willingness to take direction, and candidates had to be careful. Stark was no subtle character, and his opponents were watching for the slightest opening. They soon accused him of taking direction, allowing unnamed politicians outside the state to tell him what to do.

Moreover, it was clear that anything the president said or did would raise the ire of Senator Clark. The senior senator had been at loggerheads with the president for years. He easily had gotten himself into opposition. There is evidence that he enjoyed it. He also was a tough customer, a nasty character. He had entered the Senate the same year that Roosevelt entered the presidency, and probably considered himself the president's equal. He saw that the president was a cold fish, as self-centered as the senator, maybe more, and that riled him. Shrewd, Clark saw that the way to get Roosevelt's attention was to vote erratically and show independence. The senator was an alcoholic, drunk half the time, unpredictable, and it was easy to be erratic, by taking a drink. The calculating president could not figure him out. At that time (matters would change) Clark was secure in his Senate seat and could stick his tongue out at Roosevelt whenever he pleased. He had presidential ambitions, and when early in 1940 the president began moving openly for renomination for an unprecedented third term, it angered the senator. In championing Stark, FDR was raising a threat to Clark, who would be up for reelection in 1944. Missouri custom was for the metropolises and environs to share Senate seats, which meant that eastern Missouri took one, western the other. Stark and Clark both came from Pike County and were associated with St. Louis, and if Stark was elected in 1940 he would provide an automatic reason for the Kansas City Democrats to vote against Clark in 1944.

In the developing politics of Missouri that opened with the alliance of the president with Governor Stark and the fall of Pendergast it was at first unclear whether the senior senator would do anything for

Truman. Loyalty was not one of his virtues. Clark owed Truman at least one favor. The senior senator was lazy as he could be, and when Truman, an industrious individual, joined him in the upper house he let Truman handle all the constituent mail, not responding when constituents wrote in. But it was possible that his inaction would continue for two or three years until he roused himself when reelection time approached. Clark would take another drink. Truman's friend Easley remembered one time when the beer magnate of St. Louis, Adolphus Busch, held a Missouri party at the Shoreham Hotel, and Easley left with Jim Pendergast and Vic Messall and the Missouri politician Richard Nacy to find Senator Clark in the hall sitting in a big chair. As Easley described his condition, "He was completely stoned." Unshaven, unkempt, he needed removal from the scene as quickly as possible. Easley and friends got a bellboy and discovered where his room was and carried the chair over to the elevator and took him to his room.[2]

The senator, as Easley described things, had developed to a point where nothing seemed to matter, but when Stark became the scourge of Pendergast and in the spring of 1940 the president's friends were promoting the third term, Clark espied a challenge that shook him into action.[3] He reacted savagely when Stark (and Roosevelt, he was sure) tried to take control of the state's party machinery, initially at the party convention in St. Louis in April, then at the national convention in Chicago in July.

The *Post-Dispatch,* friendly to Stark, admitted that at the state convention fewer than four hundred delegates out of 2,597 favored Stark. In the state platform the governor's administration received the barest mention, a total of six words. The governor arrived early and seated himself in the front row on the stage, ten feet from the presiding officer, and sat grimly there as the delegates time after time hissed the mention of his name. Everything at the St. Louis session was under Clark's control, and the choice of delegates to the forthcoming Chicago convention was in Clark's hands. The senator could have excluded Stark, but graciously, it was said, allowed him to be a delegate-at-large, which meant that Stark received a half vote out of Missouri's thirty—there were twenty-six delegates, two from each congressional district, and eight delegates-at-large with half votes. Newspapers announced that Stark received his half vote because otherwise he would have been "martyrized." A sure sign of his defeat came when one or two days before the state convention Stark announced he was supporting Clark's election as chairman of the Chicago delegation. Stark was not even chosen one of the two vice-chairmen. The choice of the delegation's officers occurred at an organization meeting at the Hotel Jefferson in St. Louis on June 29.[4]

Truman was ecstatic about the way Clark lined up the delegation against the governor. "Bennett is now tearing his shirt for me," he wrote Easley.[5]

Stark then made a very large error, compounding what Clark already had considered others, by openly showing his national ambitions, both for the presidency and the vice-presidency. The governor opened headquarters in Chicago in advance of the national convention. His brother Paul began telephoning party leaders around the country urging support for the presidency if President Roosevelt did not run, and the vice-presidency if he did. When the presidency quickly became impossible the governor turned to the second choice. When he had seen the president in November of 1939 and made the arrangement to offer Truman a place on the ICC, he spoke with the president's appointments secretary, Brigadier General Edwin M. Watson, who judiciously mentioned the vice-presidency. "We think you would make a fine running mate for Chief. Couple other good ones we're looking over for V.P." Stark's rejoinder was, "I wouldn't take it with anyone but the Chief." At Chicago his supporters handed out Stark Delicious apples. On stationery of the Stark Club of Chicago, delegates were invited to "Drop in at your state headquarters and have one of the big Stark Delicious apples waiting there for you. This fruit is sent to you with our compliments and best wishes." To Missouri supporters the governor carefully stated his position: "I am not expecting to be offered the vice-presidency. I would have to cross that bridge when I came to it." His complete willingness, offered to Watson, was not known, but his headquarters activities and those of his brother were obvious.[6]

All this gave Clark opportunity, and he made the most of it. The senator released the following statement on July 10:

> Governor Stark's amazing campaign of telephonic personal solicitation for the Vice-Presidency and/or Presidency appears to be in full blast in all parts of the country except Missouri. It is probably the first time in history that anyone ever attempted to

run for President or Vice-President by employing the methods usually adopted in races for constable. Of course, I am not authorized to speak for the Missouri delegation upon this subject until the delegation has caucused. However, within the last few days Governor Stark was overwhelmingly defeated by the delegation for the minor and purely honorary and nominal post of Honorary Vice-President of the convention—an officer whose only function is to have his name printed in the convention book. For this office Governor Stark mustered only five votes out of thirty—including his own vote.[7]

After these observations it was a matter of time for Clark to come out for Truman. Years later Messall, with whom Truman by then had broken, told a story of how he, Vic, got Clark on Truman's bandwagon. According to the story Messall found Clark at the Carroll Arms Hotel in Washington, across from the Senate Office Building. He asked him why he did not make speeches for Truman. Clark said, "Why in the hell should I make any speeches for him? He never made any for me." Messall insisted that Truman made speeches and said he could give dates. They went up to Clark's office and Clark got out a bottle. Messall tried to get away, and suggested that the senator lie down and sleep. He went back to the hotel and found Senator Hatch, who said, "My gosh you look like you've lost your last friend. What's the matter?" Messall told him he had been talking to Clark. Hatch said he thought he could do something. He called Clark on a hotel phone and went over to Clark's office, and after a while returned and said Clark would speak for Truman. "I don't know what he did or said, but two weeks later Clark went to the Mayfair Hotel in St. Louis and called up everybody he knew in Missouri for Truman."[8]

It was a good story, but did not really make sense, for it sounded as if Messall was enlarging his campaign achievements to get back in Truman's good graces. More to the point was what one of the Bootheel leaders, a young attorney who became a federal judge, Roy W. Harper, told a historian from the Truman Library. Harper said that after the Chicago convention he and the other principal leader of the Bootheel, the prosecuting attorney of New Madrid County, J. V. Conran, talked to Clark, "and we told him the facts with respect to the campaign." Harper was very close to Clark, and if the senator needed any prodding, he could have done it.[9] Within days Clark was after Stark in his witty, droll way. Postmaster General

Farley resigned, and a rumor started in Missouri that Stark was a candidate for the office. It took little imagination to guess what faction of the Missouri Democrats started the rumor. Clark seized the occasion, announcing that he had read "with great interest and some amusement and surprise" that Stark was accusing him of starting the rumor. "Until I read the Governor's denial of his candidacy," said the senator,

> I was not aware that there was a vacancy in that office or that it had been suggested by anyone that he would be the proper person to fill it. If I had known that vacancy existed, as he seems to think, I would, of course, not have been surprised to learn that he was a candidate for the office outside Missouri while vehemently denying his candidacy in the state. The same thing, of course, would apply to the secretaryship of agriculture, the chairmanship of the Democratic national committee or any other good plum in sight.

Clark then asserted, and it must have been true, that when Secretary of the Navy Claude Swanson died in 1939 he, Clark, had received a telegram from the governor asking him quietly to investigate Stark's chances of being appointed, with Clark to telegraph him aboard Admiral J. K. Taussig's flagship at Bellingham, Washington, before July 6 (the governor apparently was about to take another navy cruise, and Clark was not above pointing out that fact). Clark wired the governor that he had made discreet inquiries and learned that he was not being considered. "If the governor has forgotten this incident," Clark orated, "I will be glad to make available the original message which I still have."[10]

As the senior senator thought about what Stark was doing, he warmed to his subject. Five days before the primary he offered a detailed analysis. Stark, he said, asked Pendergast in 1932 for support for the governorship and did not receive it, and agreed to manage Francis Wilson's campaign in Pike County, "losing the county which by all the rules of the game Wilson was entitled to carry." In the next years Stark licked Pendergast's boots until he obtained the boss's support in 1936. It never had been proved, Clark said, that in the senatorial election of 1934 Truman took a single fraudulent vote but "the fact that a great number of fraudulent votes were cast for Gov. Lloyd C. Stark in 1936 has been proved on hundreds of occasions in the federal court and is a matter of legal record." The governor was dumber than an oyster about the ghost votes in 1936.[11]

Stark's acceptance of Pendergast's ghost votes in 1936 reminded Clark of the contemporary scene, which he begged the governor to explain.

> Stark loves to talk about machines . . . the governor must know that he himself has been conducting one of the most vicious machines in the history of the state in his misuse of patronage, the "lug" on state employees, his prostitution of the liquor control department, and his exploitation of departments devoted to the neediest and most appealing of our citizens, such as old-age pensions, unemployment insurance and social security administrations.

Guards at the penitentiary and janitors in the eleemosynary institutions muttered under their breath when asked to make their "voluntary" contributions to Governor Stark's campaign fund from their pay. Perhaps if the governor explained to the small-fry of his administration what he was up to, they would have more appreciation of his putting the lug on them. They and the lower-paid clerks as well as department heads should have seen Stark's headquarters in Chicago when the governor was a candidate for the vice-presidential nomination. If they had seen the sumptuous, magnificent, and effete splendor of the Stark-for-Vice-President quarters at the Stevens Hotel, even the poorest employees would have felt repaid for their sacrifices.

To be sure, Stark could never appreciate Truman. "It is one of poor Lloyd's unfortunate delusions that he is the only honest man in Missouri—indeed in the world—and that anyone who happens to differ with him, particularly anyone who doubts that he is temperamentally and mentally suitable for service in the United States Senate is controlled by the powers of darkness and evil." Truman, as Clark described him, had served six years in the Senate and was able, industrious, patriotic, and had won distinction in several important legislative fields. Never had there been "the slightest scintilla of doubt in any quarter" of Senator Truman's integrity or patriotism.

Clark assisted Truman mightily, and so did Senator Guy B. Gillette of Iowa, chairman of the campaign investigating committee, who chose to investigate Stark's solicitations of state employees, putting the lug on officeholders. The Iowa senator let no one be unaware of what he was about, and in a press release of June 20 described an investigation from April 27 to May 31 by two of his staff members. They interviewed one hundred state employees, in most of the executive departments, from minor workers to department heads, and obtained affidavits or statements that a representative of the governor was working through the department heads to coerce them. The Gillette investigation disclosed that it had been the custom in Missouri to contribute 2 percent of annual salaries to the general Democratic state campaign fund. Employees also were being asked to contribute to the senatorial fund of Stark. "While such contributions are supposed to be voluntary," Gillette stated, "there is abundance of evidence to prove that many employees were indirectly coerced into contributing although they may not be in sympathy with the candidacy of Governor Stark for the U.S. Senate." Records, the investigators said, showed that as of May 31, twenty-eight thousand dollars were pledged, of which eleven thousand were collected. Gillette instructed his staff members to continue their work in Missouri until after conclusion of the senatorial campaign.[12]

What Gillette managed to do was question whether if elected Stark could serve. The question was not a large one, and many Missourians suspected a scare, but he raised it.

Moreover, he gave opportunity for Truman supporters to accuse the governor of more violations. Jean Gualdoni in St. Louis telegraphed Gillette: "We have further information regarding expenditures in the senatorial campaign in Missouri. Suggest investigator who made original investigation return to St. Louis for important information." A correspondent wrote Truman, who doubtless passed on the information, that State Bank Commissioner R. Waldo Holt had assessed each bank examiner forty dollars. Conran in the Bootheel wrote that the governor was using the state liquor department "in a manner that has never been done in this State." Liquor inspectors, he said, were taking licenses from people who did not support the governor, refusing applications to people who would not support him, and also using the license privilege to keep competition out of localities where persons supporting the governor desired no competitors.[13]

In the last days of the campaign Truman's supporters sent a telegram asking investigation of the governor's claim that the senator was using a slush fund.[14]

To all this Stark could only issue denials. Early during the Gillette onslaught he said, "there's no lug being put on anyone by me or my campaign committee. My specific instructions were 'any contributions from any source must be absolutely voluntary and no pressure put on anyone.' " His denials kept the issue alive.[15] Nor was his case helped by the fact that he was a wealthy man.

During the Truman campaign the perhaps single important thing the St. Louis headquarters did, in the person of Director General Berenstein, was to gather statements from senators friendly to Truman. It was a natural enterprise, and Berenstein did not deserve enormous praise, but he did the job, which neither Messall nor Canfil did. In mid-July twenty senators came out for Truman. Hatch, author of the law that forbade federal employees to support political campaigns, avowed that Truman's service on the interstate commerce committee made him "a most valuable, useful and needed senator." Vic Donahey of Ohio said, "I would cast my vote for Truman without reservation. He is the kind of a senator needed in Congress."[16]

Senators—Hatch, Barkley, Minton of Indiana, Lewis B. Schwellenbach of Washington (in the Truman administration Minton would go to the Supreme Court; Schwellenbach would become a cabinet member)—made personal appearances in Missouri. A much remarked affair was a rally for Truman in the Music Hall of the Municipal Auditorium in Kansas City on July 30, which began with a band concert, followed by an address by Hatch. "You know his life and character," Hatch said, "but I am not sure whether you in Missouri fully appreciate his fine record of constructive service and unwavering loyalty to the administration in Washington." On the platform were a score of union leaders. Truman spoke after Hatch. "There is not a senator in the United States," Truman remarked, "who wants to see this nation get into the European war." As he had done, he said he was against the draft and favored the Swiss plan. The *Kansas City Journal* praised the meeting, and Station KCMO carried its addresses.[17]

The next night, July 31, came a meeting in St. Louis at the Opera House, a large disappointment because of attendance. At the last moment the sponsors sought to persuade the auditorium manager to install a loudspeaker system to accommodate an expected overflow outside. Instead there was an audience of a little more than three hundred in a house seating 3,563. The turnout moved the *Post-Dispatch* to scorn: "A mighty mob of 300 jammed a section while untrodden aisles, unoccupied balconies and yawning spaces listened to the message."[18] For the occasion the head of the Brotherhood of Locomotive Engineers had telegraphed President Roosevelt and asked for an endorsement of Truman. The result was a reply from Press Secretary Early: "The President asks me to explain to you personally that while Senator Truman is an old and trusted friend, the President's invariable practice has been not to take part in primary contests." The best Truman could get from the White House for the meeting was a statement thanking labor for its support of the Democratic party.[19] Senator Barkley spoke to the group. A speaker in the old stem-winding style, who took a half hour to get started, he told them that Truman had been intelligent, progressive, constructive, industrious, dependable. He was followed by Truman.

But attendance at the St. Louis Opera House, dismal though it was, did not mean too much. Every campaign has to have a failure or two. What was more important was the manner in which Truman's colleagues in the Senate came to his defense, showed support, and pushed his candidacy against what they felt was an unworthy opponent. The governor's friends pointed out that the senators were not Missourians; their presence or statements constituted interference. It still was possible to see that Truman was no local representative, possessed national stature, and deserved return to the legislative body in which he had done well.

2

To the support of the senators was added a second support, which came not because of the actions of Truman's friends but out of the inabilities of one antagonist and the mere presence of the other. Governor Stark, it turned out, was a dangerous man politically. He had much support across the state. But he proved less than a perfect campaigner. He made mistakes, and eventually they redounded to Truman's favor. As for Milligan, he distinctly was third in the senatorial primary. He was less dangerous than Stark by far. And as matters developed, and this was even visible from the outset, Milligan's entrance into the campaign was in one notable respect of great value to the beleaguered Senator Truman.

Lloyd Crow Stark—Truman loved to mention that the governor's middle name was that of a very common bird—was a calculating man, and this attribute proved of advantage to the ambitious governor. Of the calculation there could be no doubt. Near the end of the senatorial campaign he wrote a correspondent in California who had given political advice that he always had thought out what he was about to do. "I have planned everything I have ever done since I was a boy," he wrote in a remarkable piece of frankness, "—not necessarily always to a definite goal but nearly always—but always, as you say, ready for the 'breaks,' ready to jump on the boat as it floats downstream."[20]

Stark was an efficient governor, far more so than the bumbling Park. His correspondence is impressive—the embossed stationery, the careful typing. He was a master of the one-or-two-sentence reply to people he wished to impress.

During his governorship there was accomplishment, including a new cancer hospital in Columbia, tightening of management in Jefferson City, and (one must give the devil his due) elimination of the ghost votes in Kansas City. Stark supported Judge Southern's campaign against crime, and took back control of the Kansas City Police Department with all its Leavenworth alumni.

But it was all too efficient, machinelike, inhuman. The truth was that the governor was a cold fellow. He had been head of a large and prosperous nursery, and was accustomed to telling people which tree to prune.

The governor was too ambitious. When Swanson died, Stark had a year and a half to finish his term. Moreover, it was not smart of him to appeal to Clark for help. Similarly, he should have avoided other federal offices.

Stark's background as a military man hurt his candidacy. Not many Missourians graduated from Annapolis, although his time at Annapolis was obscured by his shift to the field artillery, but the title of major, which he encouraged, did not help. "Captain Harry," Truman's title, was different. Truman quickly saw Stark's swagger. In the archives in Jefferson City is a piece of correspondence recently turned up that shows what Truman thought. The occasion was President Roosevelt's second inaugural, in January of 1937, just after Stark took office. The U.S. Army's chief of staff, General Malin Craig, a Missourian, called Truman's office about Stark's coming to

Washington. Stark would be accompanied by two military aides, Craig related, and the senator should stop worrying. "He will have two military aides who will have nothing to do but make him comfortable, and if they fail," one of Truman's secretaries wrote in a memo for the senator, "the General says he will do it himself. He says to tell you he is still from Missouri." Truman sent the memo to Colonel Claude C. Earp, adjutant general of Missouri, and said that at the inaugural the state could have only three cars and that he was reliably informed that the governor and staff would have reservations in the president's reviewing stand. Truman added a postscript by hand: "Here's a note from Gen. Craig. I understand the aides have instructions to do everything for the Gov. even button his pants."[21]

During the campaign Stark went around the state surrounded by uniformed Missouri colonels, and when he approached his automobile his chauffeur saluted him.

The governor took credit for anything in the vicinity of his operations, and did not hesitate to take credit for ruining Pendergast. He deserved credit, but he should have been more careful. In speeches he raised the issue. "There is only one answer," he asserted. "The decent, law-abiding, God-fearing people of Missouri—you and countless thousands like you—deserve the full credit for ridding our state of the combination of a greedy, rapacious gang of plunderers and corruptionists." But raising the issue tended to give him credit. In private letters he took credit; to a constituent he wrote, "I am most encouraged by the amazing response I have received from people all over the country in my efforts to clean up crime in Missouri."[22]

He was no public speaker. Even his friends admitted that. The same friend to whom he confessed how ambitious he had been since he was a boy gave him a little advice, that he should study public speaking. He answered that as he jumped on boats he would solve the speaking problem. "I have studied most everything but public speaking and have mastered everything I have tackled so far and I think I can do that too."

Part of his speaking problem was exaggeration. When he opened his campaign in Mexico, Missouri, he said, "I stand here today, firmly opposed to everything the Kansas City plunderbund has fostered—dope rings, protected gambling, corruption of public officials, unrestricted prostitution and other illegal activities." Nothing left to imagination. Truman was a rubber stamp in the grimy paw of the corrupt Pendergast gang.[23]

The senator's other antagonist in the primary, Milligan, similarly could have given a great deal of trouble, but his entrance into the campaign proved a positive good.

Milligan's background was far less impressive than that of Stark. His brother Tuck had turned to politics because of experiences in the army, during the war; he ran for his first term in Congress in 1920. Maurice had met Senator Robert M. La Follette of Wisconsin, who came to Richmond to make a speech. Afterward Milligan saw him sitting on the courthouse steps, introduced himself, and the two began a conversation that went on for hours. La Follette urged that he work for the people. "Young man, take the side of the people. It's the right side. It's not only the right side, it's the winning side." The younger Milligan sought the federal attorney job in 1934 through his brother, who had met Bennett Clark in the army. Maurice was at least third choice for the post. Clark had offered it to Jerome Walsh, son of Aylward's law partner, and Walsh turned it down for personal reasons. Clark sought appointment of Carl L. Ristine, but the U.S. attorney general, Homer Cummings, opposed. Finally there was a deal, whereby Cummings appointed Ristine assistant attorney general at a salary substantially higher than what Milligan received.[24]

Milligan had considerable reason for entering the Senate race. Early in 1940 the word got around that he was furious over the way Stark was taking credit for the downfall of Pendergast. Milligan and his assistants had prosecuted the vote fraud cases, and even though the outcome did not touch Pendergast the attorney was first in the field. Later credit accrued to Stark principally for something he did not speak about and Milligan knew, the tip-off from the retiring member of the BIR in Washington. Milligan, too, had done the work to break McCormack early in 1939.

Milligan opened his campaign the same day as Stark, and it became clear that he was no Clarence Darrow. His opening speech was a disaster. His voice was much worse than that of either Truman or Stark. His campaign was as dull as his slogans, one of which was "Democrats Will Win AGAIN with Milligan." His single advantage was negative: no one could accuse him of being machine-controlled: "Never during my life have I ever trod the political pathway to 1908

Main Street with my hat in my hand, nor have I ever asked or received any favor or support from Pendergast and his machine."[25]

Milligan's campaign failed from the outset, and he spent much of his time ensuring that he lost, but in one notable respect he was an enormous assistance to the senator: he divided the good-government vote. He took votes not from Truman but from Stark. He apparently had no idea that his entrance into the campaign would do this; there was a vein of naïveté about him and he believed he would win. But Truman could not have been renominated without the entrance of Milligan. When the specter of Stark was turning into near reality, just after the fall of Pendergast, Truman wrote Bess, "I don't want Milligan to run unless he and Stark run together. That would be too good." Early in 1940 the remnants of the machine and the supporters of Clark, not then cooperating against the governor, agreed that if Stark ran without Milligan, Stark would win, and if Milligan came in there would be great uncertainty. A Stark supporter, William H. Becker, later a federal judge, made an observation years later about the Milligan brothers, that Truman should have said a prayer of thanksgiving for them every night before he went to sleep, because Tuck created a three-way race in 1934 and Maurice did the same in 1940.[26]

Had Milligan not been so naive he might have done much better for himself. Had he been a subtle man he could have approached Stark in 1940 and mentioned a price for his neutrality in the primary. Stark as a friend of Roosevelt could have given Milligan whatever he wanted, an attractive appointment in Washington or perhaps a federal judgeship. Truman and his friends used Milligan. On the day of Truman's decision to send Messall to Jefferson City and file, Friday, February 2, 1940, Truman's friend Evans did something that came naturally to a Pendergast supporter who as a youth was tall for his age and began voting at the age of fourteen. Evans had known Tuck Milligan ever since he had sought a radio station franchise in 1935–1936, what became KCMO, and spent several days with him in Washington making the rounds of federal offices. It was easy to go to see the congressman, which he did that afternoon, and say as he did, "Tuck I think it would be a good idea—I think if your brother is nominated, he can be elected and would make a good senator; and I want to tell you that I will be glad to help you out with a financial contribution when your committee for his election is set up, I'll give you $500."

Tuck said, "Give it to me now, because the committee is already set up."

Tom believed the congressman's brother already had filed, but there was talk about withdrawing. In Maurice Milligan's book eight years later there was a plaintive commentary that may have referred to Evans's check, a large one for the time. "When some of Truman's own friends asked me to run," he wrote, "I took that as positive assurance of the then Senator's desire to stay out of the race."

Afterward Evans told Truman that for once he was supporting the candidate who was opposing him. The senator looked at his friend "kind of funny" and said, "What do you mean? When did you quit me?"

"Well," was the reply, "I just think Maurice Milligan will make a pretty good senator. I went over and contributed to his campaign."

"I don't want to know anything about that," was the response. "I wish a lot of my friends were off of me as much as you are. I might be elected."[27]

During the campaign Milligan spent much of his time lambasting his opponents, and in the course of it again served Truman. Anything he said about Truman had already been said by Stark, and he was downright helpful in what he said about the governor. Truman had refused to conduct a mudslinging campaign, which was probably a good idea, but then he did not need to do that because Milligan was doing it. The governor, Milligan said, "never raised his voice against corruption in Kansas City until months after federal prosecutions started." By this he meant Stark's late sponsorship of the voting commission to prune the Kansas City rolls. He said that Stark received ghost votes in the 1936 election. Truman and Stark were "in the same boat so far as having accepted support of the Pendergast machine but Truman has refused to desert the ship while the governor went overboard at the first torpedo. And now Governor Stark would have us believe he was the fellow who fired the torpedo." Milligan, like the Truman supporters, charged Stark with coercing licensed liquor dealers. He said that liquor inspectors refused to take action against violators of closing laws in an unnamed Missouri city, that they posted Stark-for-senator placards in places where liquor was sold. He announced that penitentiary guards were posting Stark placards while in uniform.[28]

Like the other candidates he announced his approval of President Roosevelt: "I concede nothing to Governor Stark or Senator Truman in admiration of the leadership of President Roosevelt. If elected I shall be proud to work for the perfection and extension of the great social and economic measures which President Roosevelt has inaugurated." But having made these helpful remarks, he added another that showed his naïveté. "The political agility of Governor Stark and Senator Truman is something to wonder at," he said. "From Thomas J. Pendergast, their political godfather, to Franklin D. Roosevelt, is a mighty long jump . . ."[29] The jump, of course, was much less than Milligan thought.

3

The third, and crucial, advantage that came to Senator Truman was an alliance between the Bootheel counties and a rising young Democratic politician in St. Louis, Robert E. Hannegan, who was willing to give his eight delivery wards to Truman in exchange for Bootheel votes for the St. Louis candidate for governor, McDaniel.

In a close election, as was the primary, the addition or subtraction of any bloc of votes can be crucial, and it is possible that other arrangements in the campaign ensured Truman's victory. Perhaps Truman's courting of Missouri's black voters in his Sedalia speech, a courting that involved saying things that seldom had been heard in Missouri, turned many black votes in favor of the senator. Consider the change of mind of the black leader in St. Louis, Jordan W. Chambers, who backed Cochran in 1934 and heartily disliked Stark. The governor held a rally in St. Louis aboard a segregated excursion boat. The black leader of St. Louis's nineteenth ward made up and distributed one hundred thousand cartoons showing Stark aboard a boat, standing under a sign that read, "No Negroes Allowed." That summer of 1940, perhaps sensing that because Truman came from Independence, a segregated town where blacks "knew their place" and worked as domestics and handymen for the town's householders, Chambers was about to go to Milligan, until a week before the election he talked over race relations with Truman. He went to Truman. The senator made a speech in front of Chambers's funeral parlor.[30]

To be sure, the pattern of black migration since before World War I favored the Democrats, and Truman could take advantage of it.[31] The urbanization of many outstate Negroes, and movement into the state of nearly one hundred thousand blacks in the two decades from 1910 to 1930, raised the possibility, for the first time, of a black vote. Migrating blacks increased St. Louis's black population from forty-four thousand to eighty-two thousand from 1910 to 1925. In the same period Kansas City's black population increased from twenty-four thousand to thirty-four thousand, enough in the second ward to come to the attention of Pendergast's man Cas Welch, who with increasing lack of care voted his constituents dead or alive, all the while being careful to be fair to those who really voted. At the end of the 1920s the two major cities in Missouri contained 60 percent of the state's quarter of a million black citizens. Of Missouri's counties, 102 experienced an absolute decline in black residents as blacks moved to the metropolises. The only part of the state where the black population increased, other than St. Louis and Kansas City, was the Bootheel, where intensive cultivation of cotton (there was no infestation of boll weevils) brought migrants, raising numbers from nine thousand to twenty-seven thousand. At the outset the migration largely in the cities favored the Republican party, but with attention given blacks by Democratic machines in the cities there was Democratic voting, and when the Hoover presidential strategists in 1928 sought to break into the Solid South, and did so in the border states, more Missouri blacks went over to the Democrats, and what few did not deserted the party of Lincoln during the Depression and New Deal.

Truman was sensitive to black voters even though those in Kansas City constituted a smaller portion of the population than in most cities. When he ran for presiding judge he had to campaign in the entire county, not just in largely white Independence and its lily-white environs. In his run for the Senate in 1934 he saw the advantage of Pendergast's liberal policies toward Kansas City's black community. An astute student of the later president's "conversion," as he puts it, to a liberal point of view for America's black citizens writes that it began during his first term as presiding judge and was a result of political expediency, a sense of fairness, and contact with Kansas City's black leaders, especially Chester A. Franklin, publisher of the *Kansas City Call* (whose editor in the 1920s, Roy Wilkins, was much more liberal, and later became head of the National Association for the Advancement of Colored People in New York City). By 1928 blacks made up one-third of the county payroll, many in white-collar jobs. A powerful figure among Missouri blacks, Franklin supported Truman in 1939–1940.[32]

Interestingly, the student of Truman's move toward liberal racial views believed that Truman in 1940 carefully limited his civil rights remarks to black audiences, in particular the black press. This way, so Franklin advised him, he could avoid a backlash from whites. "As implausible as this may sound, it explains Truman's actions in the 1940 campaign . . ."[33] But this judgment may not have been true, even if Franklin and Truman gave voice to it in correspondence. After all, Truman set out his liberal racial views in of all places Sedalia, a railroad town. More to the point, he allowed the union editor of *Labor* to repeat his calls to action in the Sedalia speech in the half-million-copy publication of the special issue, the single most important statement of Truman's views offered to Missourians during the campaign.

In calculating what took Truman's primary campaign to victory in 1940, it is possible to contend that he picked up many black votes. Eighty-eight percent of Missouri's blacks had given him their votes in 1934. It is difficult, however, to be sure of their importance as the single factor that put him over.

Similarly, it is difficult to be sure of the importance of votes gathered in the southwestern portion of the state by Truman's friend Easley, who after the election was proud of the nearly nine-thousand-vote plurality with which Truman carried the area around Joplin. Easley was rightly proud of the fact that after Truman became a senator the twenty-three counties in southwestern Missouri were favored with much patronage. "And Mr. Truman was religiously faithful about seeing that our area was properly considered whenever any patronage in the territory came up." One time the senator took a group from Easley's area to see the national WPA administrator, Harry Hopkins, who then was staying in the Lincoln bedroom of the White House, where he was recovering from a serious operation. Hopkins promised southwestern Missouri attention, which it received: the Jayhawk Ordnance Plant, airport improvement, road and bridge building, construction of Camp Crowder. The southwestern Missouri votes, however, probably did not prove the swing votes in the 1940 primary. Truman basically kept the allegiance of voters in that area.

Southwestern Missouri did help in one special way, a pushing into action of the mayor of St. Louis, Bernard F. Dickmann, who was inclined to let his ward leaders vote their constituents in such ways as suited their fancies. "And I told him," Easley remembered years later, "there was a possibility that the people down here who were lined up for McDaniel were going to swing to [the outstate Democrat, Allen] McReynolds, unless they got some kind of positive information out of St. Louis that he had an interest in the Senator." Dickmann thereafter became a fountain of information about how his wards were swinging toward Truman. After the primary the senator thanked Easley profusely for his good work, saying he could not thank him enough. But Truman was careful about what the southwest had done in St. Louis, writing that the city leaders had come in because of pressure and yet not entirely from Easley's group of counties. "At least, you started it," he wrote.[34]

The senator had support from Jean Gualdoni. A huge bear of a man, Gualdoni presided over a machine inside the twenty-fourth ward, the largest ward in the city. Gualdoni ran the Fairmount Democratic Club on "the Hill," as the Italian district was known, and his several precincts swayed the ward's vote. "It's not the percentage that counts so much," Gualdoni contended, "as it is where there is a certain group that stands as a bloc, a bloc that votes together. That's what made the Italians!" He controlled two hundred city jobs. In 1934 when Cochran received 104,265 votes in St. Louis, Gualdoni supported Truman and gave him half his St. Louis total of 3,742. In 1940, Milligan talked at length with Gualdoni and received the impression he would support him, but the leader had pledged to Truman. When Truman won, the ward gave him a seven-thousand-vote plurality. In seven key Hill precincts he outpolled Stark 4,925 to 450.[35]

Still, despite Truman's attraction to Missouri blacks, and to residents of the nearly forgotten (until Truman's work in the Senate) people of the twenty-three counties in southwestern Missouri, and to Gualdoni, it does seem that the arrangement the Bootheel leaders made with Hannegan was crucial to Truman's victory. Unlike the other blocs of voters that the senator might have lost, and managed to keep, the St. Louis votes provided by Hannegan were unexpected. They were new, their appearance nothing less than providential.

The Bootheel Democrats were a loose group of seven counties in which local offices were handled one way and statewide offices another. For the latter the counties' votes could be put up for bargaining, with the area's leaders touting the virtues of individuals they chose to support. In New Madrid County, J. V. Conran was the chairman, and there the Democrats depended upon him for statewide advice. For county offices they did not give much attention to him, and took their own course. "J. V.," as he was known, dealt with Jefferson City and Washington. In Pemiscot County, the bailiwick of the lawyer Roy Harper, the party operated similarly. Harper's organization normally delivered 75 to 80 percent of the primary vote to the people it supported above the county level. Unlike in New Madrid, the Pemiscot Democrats did not take sides in the races for local offices. The arrangement was that locally anyone could file, and there then would be a meeting, with representatives from every precinct, and it would decide who to support.

Truman was the Bootheel choice for the Senate, and McReynolds of Carthage was the leaders' choice for governor, and the question became one of who to go to in St. Louis to gain support for Truman. Being Young Democrats, Conran and Harper sought out two St. Louis Young Democrats, the circuit clerk of the civil courts, H. Sam Priest, and his chief deputy, Alfred Fleishman. Priest was local chairman of the McReynolds-for-governor campaign. He pointed out to Conran and Harper, however, that he had no organization, could not deliver any votes, and it would be more realistic to talk to Hannegan, then chairman of the St. Louis Democratic City Central Committee, who had control of eight wards. Hannegan, he said, was supporting McDaniel and might be willing to trade.[36]

Hannegan was an attractive young man, about the same age as Conran and Harper. He was to have a meteoric rise within his party because he had the wit—the choice he made surely was not luck— to take the winning side in the senatorial primary that year. Born in 1903, he had played football for St. Louis University, received a law degree from the university in 1925, and practiced in St. Louis. He became chairman of the City Central Committee in 1933. He was boss of the twenty-first ward, and through friends had access to seven others. He would lose out in St. Louis politics in 1941 during an internal party squabble, but because of Truman's patronage would become collector of internal revenue for St. Louis the next year, and in

1943 commissioner of internal revenue in Washington. In 1944 he was named chairman of the national committee, and kept that post until 1947. When Truman assumed the presidency he made Hannegan postmaster general. After retirement from the cabinet Hannegan became president of the St. Louis Cardinals, and died in 1949.

A trade made excellent sense for both sides. For the Bootheel the Senate race was important, for the area's principal crop was cotton and it was necessary to include the Bootheel in the New Deal's cotton support program; indeed, Senator Truman had seen to its inclusion.[37] As for the St. Louis machine people, the senatorship meant little to them. The governor's office meant a great deal. Quite apart from the issue of sentiment, that McDaniel was from St. Louis, election of a governor meant extensive patronage, not only in the little jobs for the workers but also the large assignments with big fees for lawyers associated with the organization.

Hannegan's agreement to provide Truman with St. Louis votes threatened to come apart. The St. Louis leader seemed too friendly to Stark. In July, before the national convention, he offered to support Stark for the vice-presidency. "I would like to have a Missourian on the national ticket because it would be a great help to the party in the November election," he said. The statement got into the newspapers.[38] Actually, Hannegan was probably only trying to get Stark out of Missouri, into the federal government where he could do no harm. To the Bootheel people who had made their agreement for a vote trade, any sort of friendly statement about Stark was awkward, perhaps a sign that Hannegan would not go to Truman.

Another uncertainty about Hannegan was the propensity of all political leaders to be on the winning side. At the outset of the senatorial contest Milligan was a possibility, for he would not have embarrassed Senator Clark in 1944—Milligan, from Richmond, would have represented Kansas City. But Milligan's star never rose, and toward the end of the campaign Stark and Truman seemed awfully close, with Stark slightly ahead. It was tempting to go to Stark, despite the Bootheel agreement. The more so because McDaniel's rival, McReynolds, seemed to be coming up; better to win with one statewide candidate than lose with both.

Another uncertainty that affected the St. Louis leaders, including Hannegan, was the problem of having too many machine candidates. All the St. Louis candidates were machine people. Truman definitely

was; the senator refused to admit any contrition, refused to apol-
ogize, for having supported Pendergast. The machine could not
forsake its St. Louis gubernatorial candidate, McDaniel, for Mc-
Reynolds, who was not a machine man. The way out would be to
go to Stark. The St. Louis leaders were fearful of this situation. In
pushing through their man for the governorship, they needed to
avoid losing the outstate vote, which was anti-machine.

A further confusion that appeared to be sending the St. Louis
leaders back to Stark was that to champion Truman was to display
an attachment for a candidate of Kansas City, something the St. Louis
people did not like to do and were unaccustomed to doing.

Mayor Dickmann, who sometimes acted as the political voice of
St. Louis, chose not to support Truman in any large way. He said
that ward leaders in the city should handle their sample ballots any
way they wished. Dickmann would do well under the patronage
of Senator Truman; after he, like Hannegan, lost out in his city's
politics he became postmaster of St. Louis. His position in 1940 was
difficult to measure. His sister Mayme was a supporter of Stark.
The *Post-Dispatch* for July 10 showed the sister serving cider (Stark's
Delicious) at a Stark-for-Senator Club meeting at the Hotel De Soto.
A story had it that near the end of the primary campaign he asked
Gualdoni to switch to Stark, after the Italian leader printed eighty
thousand sample ballots for Truman, telling him to print new ones
and send the bill to Hannegan.[39]

Something stirred Gualdoni, and if the story was true about dis-
carding Truman ballots in favor of Stark, that would account for it.
The leader of the Hill called Mayor Sermon in Independence. Years
afterward Truman remembered that Sermon together with Fred Canfil in Kansas City called Dickmann and told him that if he did not
support Truman they would kill McDaniel's chances. It is unlikely
that whatever votes the eastern Jackson County Democrats and the
Kansas City remnants of the machine could secure would have made
a great deal of difference in the McDaniel race, but according to
Sermon, and after the initial call to Dickmann, McDaniel himself
gave his word of honor as a gentleman that St. Louis would support
Truman.[40]

Easley in southwestern Missouri sent out telegrams relating that
he understood Truman had been traded off, and that the southwestern counties were going to muster the vote for McReynolds,

and this may have helped. Easley was a loyal Truman supporter and one would have expected him to do anything he could to keep the St. Louisians in line.

At the time these exchanges were going on between Independence and Kansas City and southwestern Missouri on the one side, St. Louis on the other, there was activity between the Bootheel and St. Louis. According to Roy Harper, "a good St. Louis friend," probably Gualdoni, called him with the same message, that Hannegan's group was not going to deliver. He also had heard from Easley.[41] Hannegan on August 1 told the *Post-Dispatch* that ten wards out of twenty-eight were pledged to Stark, ten to Truman, two to Milligan, the remainder leaving the vote up to voters rather than slating. Dickmann sent telegrams to each of the ten outstate congressional districts, to chairmen of the McDaniel committees, denying that city hall was throwing support to any individual Senate candidate. Word appeared in the *Post-Dispatch* for August 4 that the machine people were about to reconsider, which was another word for double-cross. In response, so the *Post-Dispatch* claimed on August 6, the day of the primary, the courthouse-ring politicians in southeastern Missouri, that is, the Bootheel, forced a last-minute rush to Truman. According to the newspaper the ring politicians, whose ability to get out a top-heavy vote for favored Democrats was well known, warned against any departure from Truman and mentioned the possibility of "knifing" McDaniel, that is, voting against him in the November election. "The administration leaders here, it was said, yielded to this threat . . ." Fourteen sample ballots in the wards went to Truman, seven to Stark, and Milligan was out in the cold. Seven wards were open.

In actual fact, what the *Post-Dispatch* claimed to have happened was very close to the truth. Years later in an oral history Harper told the story. Upon receiving word that Stark was going to be slated, Harper telephoned Senator Clark, who was in a St. Louis hospital with a sprained muscle in his left foot. Typically, Clark, at the moment crucial to his fellow senator's political life, settled into a hospital with this minor ailment. Not many people knew where Clark was, but Harper did. He told the senior senator what was happening and pressed him into service as a messenger, a role Clark would have been good at. "Deliver a message from Conran and myself," he said, "that when we make a bargain we keep it. We're going to deliver, and they damn well better deliver because if they don't deliver and their man is nominated, we'll cut his goddamn throat in the fall."[42]

As Harper remembered, the St. Louis people were "hot as hell" about it, but they kept their word. Just a day or two before the primary, Hannegan distributed his sample ballots. They declared for Truman.

With that decision it was all over. If Hannegan had been wavering, no one perhaps will ever know. He had reason to wait until the last moment, for he could avoid countermeasures by the machine's enemies, notably the *Post-Dispatch*, which would have countered with a huge pro-Stark volley of publicity. Fifty-eight years later the St. Louis leader's sister Alice, one of his precinct workers, remembered that her brother turned everything around. Everyone had assumed that Stark was the man, no question. She was astonished when a driver came by her precinct office and threw out the big package with the ballots marked for the senator, not the governor.[43] From Hannegan's eight delivery wards Senator Truman received a magnificent 8,411 lead over Stark. When all the ballots in the state were counted, Truman had won the nomination by a plurality of 7,976 votes over Stark, out of 656,501 cast. The vote was 268,557 for Truman, 260,581 for Stark, 127,363 for Milligan.

5

Aftermath

I f there was one single time in Truman's political
career when he thought he lost, it was the night
of August 6, 1940, and most of the next day as
he contemplated what he believed was his defeat for
renomination. It was a reason for being downhearted
such as he never had known, save perhaps the months
in late 1933 and early 1934 when his years as presiding
judge of Jackson County were coming to an end. At
that time his effort to carve a friendly congressional
district out of Independence and its rural environs and
an adjoining portion of Kansas City had succeeded, but
he failed to obtain the congressional seat—Pendergast
gave it to C. Jasper Bell, the Philippine expert. He failed
to obtain the post of county collector, because Pendergast obliged the Kansas City banker William Kemper.
The possibility of getting out of politics again opened in
1939–1940, but Truman fought it, without the sponsorship of Pendergast. He had been senator from Missouri,
and on August 6–7 he thought it was over. Bess had
enjoyed Washington, where she made friends with the

senatorial wives. For her too it had been exhilarating to be in the nation's capital; for her it would be at end.

In 1933–1934 the prospect of no political future stretched over months. The second experience suddenly presented itself. Tom Evans would remember, "I never knew that man when he wasn't optimistic. I'm serious about it. All the years that I knew him, at no time did I ever know him to be a pessimist."[1] Truman almost never gave up, once he started. Evans must have forgotten 1933–1934 and especially August 6–7, 1940.

The postmaster of Independence, Edgar G. Hinde, was with the senator on election night. Hinde was "uptown" with him, meaning he was in downtown Independence, probably the post office, and Truman asked Hinde to take him to Kansas City, ten miles straight west on Van Horn Road. The two went to see Jim Pendergast, and no one was in Jim's office except one of the circuit judges, John Cook. They went to the senator's office, Room 649 in the Federal Building at Ninth and Grand, and no one was there. Everyone calculated he was beaten. Hinde took him home, to 219 North Delaware. By that time he was seven or eight thousand votes behind. The postmaster drove him in the side driveway off Van Horn and let him out, and he said, "Well, Hinie, I guess this is one time I'm beaten." Hinde said, "Aw, it's a long time till morning; you're not beat yet." The postmaster privately thought he was.[2]

Testimony varies as to what happened at the Truman house through the night. Truman's memory was that he went to bed defeated and went to sleep.[3] At 10:30, Tom Evans called from Democratic headquarters down at the election commissioners to tell him he was quite a ways down. Margaret answered the phone. "Daddy's gone to bed," she said. In the middle of the night a "fellow" from St. Louis, as Truman remembered (it was Berenstein), called him up to congratulate him, saying that the *Post-Dispatch* said he was ahead and gaining. Truman told Berenstein to stop bothering him, that he was defeated. Margaret's memory was that Berenstein called at 4 A.M. and spoke with her mother, and she slammed the receiver down on him. As for the two Truman women that night, Mayor Sermon later asserted that they both were up all night, crying. Bess Truman disputed the point but said nothing about sleeping. The next day Evans called Margaret, who admitted she had been up all night. Margaret's testimony long afterward was that

"I can still see the tears streaming down Bess's face as we went to bed."[4]

According to Margaret, next morning at breakfast or at 10 A.M. her father's lead was down from ten thousand at 4 A.M. to two thousand. Her father, she said, went to the office in Kansas City to clean up mail, came home for lunch, and his lead was up. The leads, of course, were from the radio. He listened with them.[5]

But according to Sermon, the senator called the mayor about 10 A.M. "I haven't slept a wink, my wife and daughter cried the night through," he said. He walked over to Sermon's office—the Truman house was a few blocks away. Sermon shut the door. "You're in no condition to see anybody," the mayor told him. "You look like you've been through a sausage mill. Let's go down to my house with the postmaster and do a little quiet drinking."[6]

The mayor remembered that Truman and Hinde sat in Sermon's basement and talked. It would have been a long, desolate afternoon. About 5 P.M., Evans and Orville S. McPherson, the publisher of the *Kansas City Journal*, Truman's sole newspaper support in the city, got word through to them from Mrs. Truman that they, the two, were trying to find her husband. "Do you want to see them?" Sermon and Hinde asked. "What do you think?" was the not altogether enthusiastic answer. "Let 'em come," said Truman's hosts.

Evans and McPherson came out, in the company of a lawyer whose first name was Paul. Meanwhile a city councilman, John Thice, who lived across the street (703 Proctor Place), had come over to Sermon's house (701 Proctor) and asked what was going on. Thice proposed that they all go out to his cabin on Lake Lotawana, fifteen miles southeast of Independence. Sermon and wife loaded up cars with chickens and other things to eat and the group went out to the lake.[7]

While they were at the lake the news came that Truman had won. "Then I saw him begin to nod, relaxed, he was perfectly worn out . . ." Sermon said he took him home to sleep. He was supposed to fly back to Washington on important business the next morning at nine.

Such was the immediate aftermath of the close senatorial primary of 1940, so far as concerned its principal contestant.

In moving onward after renomination, Senator Truman managed reelection in November, and the question must be what, beyond the harrowing experience in the primary, he took from the rise and fall of Pendergast and its direct consequence, the fight with Stark—what he took into his second term in the Senate and especially what he used in occupying the two highest offices of the executive branch of the United States government over the next years, the vice presidency in January through April 12, 1945, and the presidency from then onward until he left the White House on January 20, 1953.

The second term in the Senate lasted only four years, mostly the years of American involvement in World War II, and one can assume that his extraordinary achievement during that time, creation and then management of what became known as the Truman Committee, a Senate special committee to look into the war effort and discover errors of omission and commission and recommend correction, partook of the same reasonable procedures, the same careful weighing of alternatives, that he had shown with Pendergast and the boss's nemesis, Stark. The fall of the boss of Kansas City stood as an object lesson as he measured the wartime behavior of citizens, corporations, and the military. He frequently saw people attempting to achieve personal rather than public purposes. The experience with Pendergast made him far more understanding than the ordinary elected official. He had not "seen it all"; the national scene was a larger experience than what the boss and Stark had known. Pendergast visited that scene only for a few years, and Stark's connection with national affairs had been fleeting. Still, working with one of the nation's greatest political bosses, cooperating when convenient, balancing Pendergast's requests with the public interest when such was called for, proved of immense importance to the senator. After Pendergast lost power, the senator managed to withstand the machinations of a ruthless governor supported by a faithless president.

There was a similar effect on Truman's political life beginning in January 1945. The earlier years of smaller pressures provided the stamina to be a great president. Time after time in the history of American politics it is possible to see major figures, and not merely members of the House and Senate, or cabinet members, but presidents, make egregiously wrong judgments. Sometimes the errors require a long time to appear. They rise up in startling ways, making the observer wonder if there has been some mysterious personality change. Their source, to be sure, lies in basic inexperience. During his presidency Truman was capable of errors. His decision to take the country into the Korean War involved a legalistic effort to avoid a declaration of war by describing the great conflict as a police action; in June 1950 he could have obtained a declaration and should have asked for it. He allowed extension of the war into North Korea. He waited too long to relieve General Douglas MacArthur; he should have brought him home in 1945, to receive due laurels and overdue retirement. On the domestic scene in 1952 he seized control of the nation's steel industry, having been misinformed by his cabinet of the need for such action, with the result that the Supreme Court gave the companies back to their owners with a stinging rebuke to the president for acting under a claim of presidential power he did not possess. During his second term tiredness led him into defensive behavior and snappishness with opponents. But errors never overwhelmed him. He withstood them, waited them out, knowing he could continue. The adversities of his earlier political years had shown that he could. He went on to very large accomplishments, especially in foreign affairs, accomplishments that set the nation's course for the rest of the century.

Notes

Introduction
1. Lawrence H. Larsen and Nancy J. Hulston, *Pendergast!*

Chapter 1: Jackson County to Washington
1. Tom L. Evans oral history, 178.
2. The best sources for the boss of Kansas City and his machine are Larsen and Hulston, *Pendergast!*, Lyle W. Dorsett, *The Pendergast Machine,* and William M. Reddig, *Tom's Town: Kansas City and the Pendergast Legend.* The Larsen and Hulston book largely replaces that of Dorsett, a much smaller volume published before most of the collections in the Harry S. Truman Library in Independence, Missouri, became available. The collections still need consultation, notably the oral history by the county and state Democratic chairman, James P. Aylward. The Reddig volume is remarkable for accuracy, even though it is based almost exclusively on the files of the *Kansas City Star.* The book is shrewd in its judgments and the author offers them with wry humor. Rudolph H. Hartmann, *The Kansas City Investigation: Pendergast's Downfall, 1938–1939,* is an inside account of the collapse of Pendergast and the machine by the principal investigator of the Treasury Department.
3. Carolyn Pendergast called her husband and told him a policeman had come to the house and said Tom, Jr., had been kidnaped. "I didn't waste a second. I sent for two men who were pretty tough. They came to my office right away. I told them to have Tom back in two hours. One of them hesitated, said he didn't know anything about it. Well, I slapped him with my open

135

hand. The other tried to protest. I hit him with my fist and knocked him through the glass door." Spencer R. McCulloch, " 'Boss' Pendergast Tells the Story of His Remarkable Career." Pendergast's wife later telephoned and said another man, a wealthy druggist, had been kidnaped.

4. Jerome Beatty, "A Political Boss Talks about His Job," 109.

5. Hartmann, *Kansas City Investigation*, 148–53.

6. *Missouri Waltz: The Inside Story of the Pendergast Machine by the Man Who Smashed It*, 12.

7. *Chronicle of an American Crusader: Alumni Lectures Delivered at the Hebrew Union College, Cincinnati, Ohio, December 7–10, 1942*, 74. Mayerberg's mettle had appeared in 1930 when he led a movement to dismiss the president of the University of Missouri, who had dismissed a faculty member and suspended another for taking part in a student questionnaire on the subject of sex. Prominent Jewish businessmen

> solemnly urged me to remain in the background and let the Christian preachers carry on the fight. This fearsome attitude of some prominent Jews always sickens me, and I am praying for the day when all Jews will be so completely filled with the spirit of American liberty, that they will not hesitate to fulfill public responsibility without fear of reaction on the part of bigots and fanatics. I warn you that, when you are in active rabbinical service, situations will confront you which will require you to speak out as free men. Be sure you have the facts and that the facts are right; then speak honestly and courageously. But be ready and willing to receive the rebuffs of the fearful and the condemnation of wizened souls, whose latent prejudices are awakened to hostility. (80)

8. Jonathan Daniels interview with Truman, November 12, 1949, box 1, Daniels papers. Kansas City's population was 399,746, the county's 470,454.

9. October 31, 1930.

10. For the Pickwick papers see Andrew J. Dunar, *The Truman Scandals and the Politics of Morality*, 7–11.

11. The federal prosecutor, Milligan, no friend of Truman, was the source of this story: "A good friend of mine, in whose integrity and reliability I have implicit confidence, told me Pendergast had stated to him his reason for wanting his own friend in the Senate." *Missouri Waltz*, 211.

12. Franklin D. Mitchell, "Who Is Judge Truman? The Truman-for-Governor Movement of 1931," 3–15.

13. "My impressions of the Senate, the House, Washington, etc.," undated. "Biographical Material," box 168, Senate–Vice President file.

14. The archives of the State of Missouri in Jefferson City in 1998 accessioned the papers of a former secretary of state, Charles U. Becker, in whose correspondence was a letter testifying to Truman's awkward personal position early in 1934. It related organization of the Natural Rock–Asphalt Company in Kansas City, in which the then presiding judge was to possess 10 percent of the no-par-value stock. Capital was set at three

thousand shares totaling $30,000. An unnamed party was to put in $1,000 cash, to be paid back out of the first profits of the company; meanwhile he was to be assigned 10 percent of the stock. L. C. Miller to Becker, January 13, 1934. Miller wrote that he had gone over the entire proposal with Truman, who in turn conferred with "Mr. T. J." The latter "endorsed the proposition and gave his consent and approval."

15. James P. Aylward oral history, 60.

16. McCulloch, " 'Boss' Pendergast Tells the Story of His Remarkable Career."

17. Robert H. Ferrell, *Harry S. Truman: A Life,* 412.

18. The present writer finds the alternative account of Pendergast and FDR much more convincing. The basis for the contention that the boss and the later president had made an agreement in 1931 is a conversation between Farley and Senator Bennett Champ Clark, attested to by Clark in a letter to Reed in 1933. Clark, who in 1932–1933 was anti-Pendergast, did not believe Farley. It is likely that the latter, making the explanation, was attempting to justify patronage to Pendergast, who seemed a more useful supporter of the administration. See J. Christopher Schnell, "Missouri Progressives and the Nomination of F.D.R.," 270n. Farley repeated the point in his books of 1938 and 1948. In the former year it would have made Pendergast feel good. In 1948 he had broken with Roosevelt, Pendergast and FDR were dead, Truman was president, and it was a pleasant thing to say. In regard to the movement of Missouri's delegates to Roosevelt, it seems more likely that a group of Wilsonian progressives that included Ewing Y. Mitchell, William Hirth, Eldridge Dearing, and Gualdoni led the way. (For Mitchell see below; Dearing was from southeast Missouri.) Of this group it is quite possible that Mitchell took the initiative in communicating with the Roosevelt forces. Gualdoni possessed the most political power. Schnell, ibid. The interesting aspect of all this, of course, is that later, when Roosevelt sided with Governor Stark against Pendergast, it might have been in part because of resentment over Pendergast's support of Reed in 1932. Years afterward a Missouri congressman appointed by Truman to the federal bench, Judge Richard Duncan, told a friend shortly before he died that FDR hated Pendergast, and that it went back to the time when the boss supported Reed. According to the judge, when Truman asked Roosevelt for a pardon for Pendergast, who reportedly was dying in Leavenworth, FDR replied with an obscenity. John K. Hulston, *An Ozarks Lawyer's Story: 1946–1976,* 90. As for the threat of a fistfight between Pendergast and Gualdoni, it is unbelievable. The gym owner and boxing-wrestling referee and trainer who handled Gualdoni thought his protégé might become a champion, but the dream was shattered when the fighter met Dora Boroni of Joliet. Boroni told him it was either boxing or her, he could not have both; he chose her. Later at the national convention in New York in 1924, Gualdoni asked some Ku Klux Klan people on the floor if they had credentials. When they attacked him he knocked out two and hit the third in the stomach so hard that, so said a newspaper article, "You couldn't see Gualdoni's fist, it was buried so far into the man's stomach." Interview with Jean Gualdoni's son, Louis C. Gualdoni, Sr., St. Louis, July 20, 1998. According to the *St. Louis Post-Dispatch,*

June 27, 1932, when Gualdoni asked at the caucus if a proposed vote to commit the delegates would bind him if he were present, and was told it would, he started for the door. He hesitated when Pendergast shouted after him, "I'll just go along with you." The Kansas City boss followed him into the hall, where he said: "You're one of these tough guys. I have my own way of taking care of a fellow like you." Gualdoni glanced about the corridor and saw a group of Pendergast followers from Kansas City in strategic positions. He walked toward an elevator while saying, "I'm not arguing with you now, Tom," with emphasis on the "now."

19. Aylward oral history, 60–61.

20. Ibid., 63–64.

21. Monroe to Jonathan Daniels, September 29, 1949, "Daniels, Jonathan . . . ," box 298, president's secretary's files.

22. Aylward oral history, 87.

23. "My impressions of the Senate, the House, Washington, etc.," box 168, Senate–Vice President file.

24. Aylward oral history, 94.

25. Jonathan Daniels, *The Man of Independence,* 170.

26. Park to William Job, July 7, 1934, quoted in Gene Schmidtlein, "Truman's First Senatorial Election," 143.

27. Schmidtlein, "Truman's First Senatorial Election," 146.

28. Ferrell, *Harry S. Truman,* 132.

29. A. Theodore Brown and Lyle W. Dorsett, *K.C.: A History of Kansas City, Missouri,* 201.

Chapter 2: Collapse of the Machine

1. The decision already had been taken. Aylward and Jim Pendergast went to St. Louis and saw or telephoned such members of the state committee as they could, and lined people up in favor of Park. They went back to Kansas City and talked to Tom Pendergast. While they were in Pendergast's office Stark called, and despite Pendergast's having told the major at the time of Wilson's choice that he would support him four years later, Stark said he still wanted to run. The boss said, "All right." Then he told Aylward and Jim, "You don't have to keep my word to him." Aylward oral history, 47.

2. To George R. Collins, February 18, 1935, "C," box 114, president's secretary's files.

3. *Whistle Stop* 12, no. 3 (1984).

4. To James E. Murray, February 10, 1951, "Wheeler, Burton K.," box 328, president's secretary's files. Murray was senator from Montana.

5. Daniels interview with Truman, November 12, 1949, p. 58, box 1, Daniels papers.

6. The role of Farley in this affair is not very clear. Years later, when the postmaster general had broken with Roosevelt, he told an interviewer that on the way back from Senator Robinson's funeral he promised Harrison and Barkley, in the presence of two other senators, not to intervene. According to him, FDR asked him to break his word in regard to Dieterich and he refused. "And I went to the White House when I got off the train and told Roosevelt. I issued a statement, as I recall it, stating that as Chairman of the National

Democratic Committee I wouldn't interfere, and he had permitted me to use that. But that night when he called me he wanted me to break my word, and I said, 'I wouldn't break my word, Mr. President, for you or anybody else.' And he got hold of Kelly, and Kelly got hold . . . Harry Hopkins, and they got Dieterich . . ." James A. Farley oral history, May 19, 1976, by Bill Cooper, 27–28.

7. Daniels interview with Truman, November 12, 1949, p. 58, box 1, Daniels papers.

8. January 20, 1936, no. 497, box 18, miscellaneous historical documents; May 20, ibid.; to Fred Canfil, March 16, ibid.

9. Robert H. Ferrell, ed., *Dear Bess: The Letters from Harry to Bess Truman, 1910–1959,* 395.

10. Folder 7226, Stark papers.

11. Letter of November 22, 1937, box 10, general file, pertaining to family, business, and personal affairs.

12. Letter of November 23, ibid.; letter of December 7, Ferrell, ed., *Dear Bess,* 408.

13. Aylward oral history, 6.

14. Ibid., 7.

15. *St. Louis Post-Dispatch,* October 6, 1936, vertical file; Barrett to Willis A. Musseter, November 27, 1936, folder 1605, Barrett papers.

16. Alfred Steinberg, *The Man from Missouri: The Life and Times of Harry S. Truman,* 151.

17. For Fennelly's observation see Herbert Kelley, "Youth Goes into Action," 112. Years later, in the early 1970s, Thomas J. Pendergast, Jr., raised another explanation for the vote frauds of 1936. Having just read Margaret Truman's biography of her father, he drafted a letter to her, never sent, in which he not merely criticized her father for not supporting his father when the machine got into trouble but also claimed that the deceased president earlier had backed Boss Tom's brother Mike, who died in 1929, and thereafter Mike's son Jim, and was essentially disloyal to the boss. Rivalry between Tom and Mike, so Tom, Jr., wrote, reached back to the last days of Alderman Jim in 1910–1911, after whose death the ward bosses chose Tom over Mike as the alderman's successor. Tom, Jr., who himself had taken no part in the machine but must have been privy to his father's thinking on many matters, espied a conspiracy against his father that included young Jim, who carefully undermined Boss Tom by bringing in his own man as successor to a secretary of the boss who had taken ill in the mid-1930s. In 1936, according to Tom, Jr., Jim wanted to take over from Boss Tom, who was too ill that year to manage the machine, and used the election as an opportunity to show he could bring out the vote. "JP till the day he died would never admit to anyone that he was to blame. But he knew and his conscience must have told him day and night till the day he died that he alone was responsible for the downfall of the P.O. [political organization]." Folder 7, Thomas J. Pendergast, Jr., papers. Young Tom bitterly resented the appearance of Truman, then vice president, at the funeral of his father early in 1945, and in his proposed letter pointed out that Truman later broke with Jim Pendergast but came to his funeral too.

18. Maurice M. Milligan, *Missouri Waltz: The Inside Story of the Pendergast Machine by the Man Who Smashed It*, 149.

19. Annotation by Truman to Frank McNaughton and Walter Hehmeyer, *This Man Truman* (New York: McGraw-Hill, 1945), 82, Truman Library.

20. Larsen and Hulston, *Pendergast!* 169.

21. Milligan, *Missouri Waltz*, 165.

22. Farley diary, November 19, December 3, 1937.

23. 75th Cong., 3d sess., *Congressional Record*, vol. 83, p. 2, February 15, 1938, vertical file.

24. Letter of February 21, 1938, *Kansas City Star*, September 15, 1978, vertical file. There has been some question of the provenance of the Leib letter, but to the present writer it seems genuine. Truman's papers for his first senatorial term were deposited in the Treasury Building in Washington and disappeared; hence there is no way to prove that Truman sent such a letter.

25. Letters of June 17, 1935, October 29, November 25, 1937, box 10, general file, pertaining to family, business, and personal affairs.

26. Hartmann, *Kansas City Investigation*, 69.

27. Editorial, March 29, 1940, vertical file.

28. Larsen and Hulston, *Pendergast!* 135.

29. McCulloch, " 'Boss' Pendergast Tells the Story of His Remarkable Career."

30. Milligan, *Missouri Waltz*, 172–73. The likely informer of the *Kansas City Star*'s Washington reporter was Charles T. Russell, deputy commissioner in charge of the income tax unit of the BIR. He became deputy commissioner in 1933 and left on February 28, 1938. Annual volumes of the *Official Register of the United States* (Washington: Government Printing Office) give legal residences in states and congressional districts. Russell was from Missouri's fifth district, that is, Kansas City. Before going to Washington he had been special agent in charge in Kansas City, and had taken part in the income tax conviction of Lazia. Moreover, in October 1937 he brought the Pendergast income tax returns to Washington. Larsen and Hulston, *Pendergast!* 210. These authors speculate that Russell might have been uncertain of the trustworthiness of agents in the field, which may well have been true. It is also possible that, knowing what had happened in Chicago, he was attempting to do something about it. The fact that he brought in the records makes it more likely that upon leaving the BIR he was the individual who talked to the reporter.

31. J. Christopher Schnell, "New Deal Scandals: E. Y. Mitchell and F.D.R.'s Commerce Department," 363–65, 371–73. Newspaper reports indicated a meeting in New York of Postmaster General Farley, Congressman Bell, Senators Truman and Clark, and Pendergast. Mitchell was bitter about his experiences, and publicized them as best he could. After he left the administration he turned Republican. His case against his chief in the department of commerce, Secretary Roper, was understandable. President Roosevelt's postmaster general in 1940–1945, Frank C. Walker, in the early 1930s executive secretary of the Executive Council, an organization to coordinate the cabinet departments and the new independent agencies, found Roper a trial:

Then there was Dan Roper, secretary of commerce, who attended
the sessions of the Executive Council with regularity. I can still
hear Dan, when his opinion was asked about some new policy or
idea, responding with the same hackneyed reply: "Mr. President,
I have just appointed a committee to study and report on the
matter. I am sure they will go into it thoroughly and bring us a
very intelligent report."

Robert H. Ferrell, ed., *FDR's Quiet Confidant: The Autobiography of Frank C.
Walker,* 90–91.

32. Lyle W. Dorsett, *Franklin D. Roosevelt and the City Bosses,* 103.

33. When Morgenthau left the Treasury Department he removed a mas-
sive collection of documents, which has been added to over the years.
The Morgenthau papers are in two parts, the first of which has been denominated the diaries and is in consecutively numbered "books," each
comprising several hundred pages. The diaries have been filmed, in 250
reels. A search of the first portion of the diaries, for 1933–1939, reels 5–49,
April 1936 to April 1939, offered no evidence of the president's knowledge
of the Pendergast bribe until June 8, 1938 (p. 122, book 128, reel 35). The
president telephoned at 1:20 P.M. and the secretary said, "Henry talking.
Surely. Oh, no, I was just thinking. Is he (Governor Stark) going to be here?
How late will he be here? Half past six. I will buy his apple trees. (Laughs)
I see. Well, I am coming over at 2 o'clock. You will tell me at two. I gather
you have company now." This was the entire recorded conversation, with
nothing of what the president said. Morgenthau later wrote: "Governor
Stark of Missouri brought this matter to the President's attention. He wants
to know what we can do to 'get' this fellow Pendergast. He claims that
Pendergast has received $500,000 out of the Missouri insurance case." In
addition to the diaries there is a general file of 1,187 boxes. A search of
its finding aid revealed nothing on Pendergast, save boxes 386 and 388.
In the former were two small memoranda, in the latter the manuscript of
Hartmann's *Kansas City Investigation.* Box 514 contains memoranda of the
secretary's conversations with the president, and has been filmed in two
reels and denominated the Morgenthau diary; it begins in January 1938 and
runs to 1945, but has no memos for some conversations, notably that of
June 8, 1938, mentioned above. It has nothing on Pendergast.

34. Elmer L. Irey and William J. Slocum, "How We Smashed the Pendergast Machine," 67–76; Irey and Slocum, *The Tax Dodgers: The Inside Story of
the T-Men's War with America's Political and Underworld Hoodlums,* 225–44.
The article and book are the only sources for Irey's part in the Pendergast
investigation. Because of a recent law, income tax records of the Treasury
Department are virtually inaccessible. Many BIR investigations also seem
to have left no records.

35. Larsen and Hulston, *Pendergast!* 9.

36. Milligan, *Missouri Waltz,* 198; Reddig, *Tom's Town,* 317, 321. See also
Larsen and Hulston, "Criminal Aspects of the Pendergast Machine," 168–
80. The latter authors relate that "All monies from an annual motor vehicle
tax paid to the city revenue collector went directly into Pendergast's coffer.

In addition, all honest businesses in Kansas City paid five to ten percent of their annual gross incomes to the machine" (171). The figure for businesses seems high, impossibly so in view of Pendergast's willingness to chance the insurance companies' bribe of 1935–1936.

37. Memorandum by E. Kemp to the attorney general, March 28, 1939, reel 115, Murphy papers; Kemp to Murphy, March 30, reel 51; pp. 181, 183, 186, book 171, reel 46, Morgenthau diaries.

38. Folder 6280, Stark papers. Within the Treasury Department, feeling against Murphy and Hoover was considerable. Irey received a letter from his agent in Kansas City, presumably Hartmann, that the treasury men there were laying bets that Hoover would be on the ground as soon as matters heated up. The day after the agent wrote, Hoover appeared. The Washington bureau chief of the *Post-Dispatch*, Raymond P. Brandt, told a treasury man that the case was 99 percent Internal Revenue and that everyone in Missouri was laughing "about how Frank and J. Edgar flew out there to be on the ground when something happened, obviously to grab the glory." P. 212, book 176, reel 48, Morgenthau diaries.

39. Milligan, *Missouri Waltz*, 197.

40. Larsen and Hulston, *Pendergast!* 124.

41. Hartmann, *Kansas City Investigation*, 131.

42. Farley diary, March 28, July 20.

> We got around to Governor Stark and the President said somehow or other he did not know much about Stark. I told the President that personally I was very much incensed at Stark because at the time of the Pendergast investigation, I had a visit from James [Michael] Pendergast's son who was accompanied by a friend and I was asked to intercede. I told Pendergast at the time that the case had to take its course and if no one were involved, there was nothing to worry about, but in any event I could do nothing because the Department of Justice and the Treasury Department were handling it and there was just nothing I could do. I told the President I did not call anyone in on this case. I went on to say that some days afterwards I received a call from Stark and he intimated to me that I had interfered or was interfering in this matter. I said I was not interested in that or any other similar case and I resented Stark's intimation that I had been interested. The President said Stark called him on the telephone, indicating he was dissatisfied with the way the Treasury Department was proceeding with the investigation. The President told Stark that the Treasury Department was proceeding along regular lines and there was nothing to worry about. I wanted the President to understand my status and that I was in no way interfering in this or any other case. He said he understood perfectly.

Farley diary, July 23. At this time Farley was angling for the presidential nomination, in the event Roosevelt did not run for a third term, and was being very careful in what he said in his conferences with FDR.

43. William P. Helm, *Harry Truman: A Political Biography*, 99.
44. Richard Lawrence Miller, *Truman: The Rise to Power*, 311–12.
45. Milligan, *Missouri Waltz*, 231.

Chapter 3: Organizing and Campaigning
1. Letter of February 21, 1937, box 10, general file, pertaining to family, business, and personal affairs.
2. Letter of July 9, 1938, "Correspondence File, Truman, Harry S.," box 2, Messall papers.
3. Truman to Bess W. Truman, July 7, box 10, general file, pertaining to family, business, and personal affairs; August 9, Ferrell, ed., *Dear Bess*, 418.
4. Truman to Bess W. Truman, August 9, ibid., 418.
5. Folder 7331, Stark papers.
6. To Harry Easley, January 13, 1940, "Easley, Harry, Jan.–June, 1940," box 2, Easley papers.
7. Easley oral history, 44–45.
8. Daniels interview with Sermon, p. 22, box 1, Daniels papers.
9. Sermon to Easley, February 20, Easley to Sermon, March 19, "Easley, Harry, Jan.–June, 1940," box 2, Easley papers.
10. Evans oral history, 250–51.
11. Helm, *Harry Truman*, 127.
12. "Campaign, Senatorial 1940," box 51, Senate–Vice President file.
13. Easley oral history, 18–19; Harry H. Vaughan oral history, 38. Evans disliked Canfil; he admitted his loyalty but thought him not merely odd but inconsequential. Oral history, 469ff.
14. Easley oral history, 49–50.
15. For belief that Messall, Berenstein, and even Canfil took money see letters in Ferrell, ed., *Dear Bess*, 443–44, 446, 476, 478; Evans oral history, 273–77. He first may have heard about Messall from the operator of his sound truck, John A. Earp, who had an interesting story. Earp said that the senator's secretary dealt with one of Earp's competitors in Jefferson City who desired the sound job, that the competitor attempted to pay the secretary but Earp received the job from Canfil in Kansas City and did not pay for it. "Some time later, after the campaign, this individual in Jefferson City came by to see me and asked what the job cost me. During the general campaign [for the November election] this secretary disappeared. He was out, I don't know why." John A. and Vernia Earp oral history, 12–13.
16. Vaughan oral history, 31.
17. Lewis T. Barringer oral history, 7.
18. Harry H. Vaughan, "Looking Back with Gen. Harry Vaughan," 197.
19. Snyder oral history, 48–50.
20. An anonymous account in the Byrnes papers, folder 640, relates that Truman told the senator he had no money for a campaign and asked if Byrnes would enlist Baruch. The latter, according to this testimony, disapproved of President Roosevelt's attempts in 1938 to purge Democratic senators uncooperative with the administration and made two contributions. The same story has it that Bennett Clark told Byrnes that he, Clark,

obtained a third. Jordan A. Schwarz, *The Speculator: Bernard M. Baruch in Washington, 1917–1965,* 368, states that Baruch gave four thousand dollars.

21. Evans oral history, 269–71; "Truman, Harry S., 1940–1963 (folder 1)," box 5, Evans papers.

22. "Harry S. Truman Campaign Data," box 61, president's secretary's files.

23. Easley to Truman, July 7, 1939, "Easley, Harry, 1939," telegram, Easley to E. M. Hayes, deputy WPA administrator, Jefferson City, September 16, 1939, "Easley, Harry, 1939," box 1, Easley papers; the conversation with Casteel is in Truman to Frank H. Lee, January 4, 1940, "Lee, Frank H. Hon.," box 74, Senate–Vice President file; Truman to Casteel, "Easley, Harry, Jan.– June, 1940," box 2, Easley papers; Roosevelt's note is in "President's Memos (Original, Apr. 6, 1940)," box 14, Watson papers; Tracy to Truman, "WPA," box 224, Senate–Vice President file.

24. "Scrapbook of clippings," box 10, Messall papers.

25. "Daily reports, July 8–August 5, 1940," box 10, Messall papers.

26. A copy of the one-and-one-half-cent letter is in "Easley, Harry—Jan.– June, 1940," box 2, Easley papers. Vaughan's oral history, 31–32, and his unpublished memoirs, "Whipping Boy—First Class," p. 9, box 2, Vaughan papers, relate receipts as eight hundred dollars.

27. A copy of Bulletin No. 1 is in "Scrapbook of clippings," box 10, Messall papers.

28. *St. Louis Post-Dispatch,* June 16, 1940.

29. Attendance may have been increased by an action of the Young Democrats, about which Messall's assistant, Catherine Bixler, learned. "The Young Democrats are planning to have a dance the same night as our meeting, in the Convention Hall in the Park. They are going to get a name band, and they are sparring with Don Bestor and Art Castle now. They can get an awfully good price on Art Castle. They figure that the dance will bring an extra thousand people to Sedalia, but of course there is to be no avowed connection between the Y. D. dance and our meeting." Bixler to Messall, May 28, "Bixler, Catherine," box 1, Messall papers.

30. *Kansas City Star,* July 4.

31. The editor of the newspaper initially agreed to send out a thousand copies of the current issue by using Truman's campaign mailing list. In a telegram of March 19, Messall said he spoke to the editor about a special edition in July and the editor thought it could be arranged. "Labor (newspaper)," box 73, Senate–Vice President file.

32. Copies of press releases are in box 9, Messall papers. They often quote or summarize speeches.

33. Snyder oral history, 50, 60–61, 71, 133; Faris oral history, 99.

34. No. 2, box 1, miscellaneous historical documents.

35. The New Franklin address appeared in a press release the next day; see also *Kansas City Star,* June 28.

36. The following is from the John A. and Vernia Earp oral history, 2–11, 19–25, 29.

Chapter 4: Victory

1. *Kansas City Star,* July 31, 1940.

2. Easley oral history, 22–23.

3. Ibid., 21.

4. *St. Louis Post-Dispatch*, April 16, 1940; unidentified clipping in "Scrapbook of clippings," box 10, Messall papers; *Kansas City Star*, May 3, 1940, ibid. "Stark was steam-rollered and flattened by the Clark organization, although 'generously' voted a place on the Missouri delegation." *St. Louis Star Times*, June 2, ibid.

5. Postscript in letter, July 1, "Easley, Harry—Jan.–June, 1940," box 2, Easley papers.

6. *Kansas City Star*, July 11, "Scrapbook of clippings," box 10, Messall papers; Watson papers; folder 10971, Stark papers; *Kansas City Star*, July 14. Stark's ambition for federal office is evident in his papers, and this may have been why after he left office he hesitated to open them; for years they were closed. Dale Carnegie, author of *How To Win Friends and Influence People* (1937), a native of Missouri, wrote the governor on April 25, 1939, that "It is high time we had a Missouri man in the White House—a Missouri man who knows a good apple when he sees it. So, when an organization is launched to put Governor Stark in the White House, please let me be one of the original members." Folder 11165, Stark papers. "Confidentially, may I tell you that I would not be adverse to making the race you mentioned against Mr. Dewey, and should such a race ever materialize, I have every reason to hope and believe that the outcome would be in my favor." Stark to Romaine Lowdermilk, October 13, 1939, folder 11180. "I have heard recently from sources in Washington which I consider very close to the 'throne,' that the President would not be a third-term candidate." T. A. W. Lewis, October 19, folder 11182. A few days later the governor was looking at the Department of the Navy, and wrote a correspondent that it was best not to consider that secretaryship unless the nation were about to be drawn into the war or he, Stark, were drafted, in which case he would be a good soldier. To Grant Peterson, October 23, folder 11182. "I was very much interested in the gossip Stick brought back. The lightning might strike. However, I am actively running for the Senate—but if that other thing should develop that will be something else." To Hal Stickney, January 24, 1940, folder 11197. When the vice-presidency went to Secretary of Agriculture Henry A. Wallace at the Chicago convention, Stark scrambled to get on the right side:

> Five minutes after I learned President Roosevelt favored Secretary Wallace for the Vice Presidency I issued the following statement: "It has been my contention and the contention of my supporters that a Mid-Westerner should be nominated as Vice President. My friends had planned to place my name in nomination before this convention, but we are anxious to make the nomination for the Vice Presidency harmonious. I think that my friend, Secretary Henry Wallace, has great strength and the support of the farmers. He will make an ideal candidate for the Vice Presidency, and I am happy to withdraw in his favor. I, therefore, have requested my friends not to place my name in nomination."

To Edwin M. Watson, July 19, folder 7331.

7. Folder 364, Clark papers.

8. Daniels interview with Messall, October 27, 1949, pp. 52–53, box 1, Daniels papers.

9. Harper oral history.

10. *Daily Capitol News,* July 10, 1940, box 11, Messall papers.

11. For these and the following Clark remarks see folder 165, Clark papers; *Daily Capitol News,* August 2, 1940, box 11, Messall papers; *St. Louis Post-Dispatch,* August 2; *Kansas City Star,* August 4.

12. "Gillette Investigation Committee," box 61, Senate–Vice President file; *St. Louis Post-Dispatch,* June 21, 1940.

13. Gualdoni to Gillette, n.d., "Gillette Investigation Committee," box 61, Senate–Vice President file; Robert A. Cox to Truman, June 22, 1940, ibid.; Conran to Gillette, June 24, ibid.

14. Press release, August 5.

15. *Kansas City Journal,* April 19; Kenneth P. Middleton, "Political Slants," *St. Louis Star Times,* June 20, in "Scrapbook of clippings," box 10, Messall papers. U.S. Senate, 77th Cong., 1st sess., *Investigation of Presidential, Vice Presidential, and Senatorial Campaign Expenditures, 1940,* 49–51, the report of the Gillette committee, contains only a sketchy account of the Missouri investigation.

16. *Kansas City Journal,* June 9, "Scrapbook of clippings," box 10, Messall papers.

17. July 31, box 11, Messall papers.

18. August 2.

19. Margaret Truman, *Harry S. Truman,* 131.

20. To Frank Peterson, August 2, 1939, folder 11173, Stark papers.

21. Letter of January 9, 1937, 10/9, Governor Inaugurations, National Guard, 133 Adjutant General, Missouri State Archives.

22. *St. Louis Post-Dispatch,* May 19, 1940, box 12, Messall papers; Stark to Mrs. Ben H. Sanders, June 9, 1919, folder 11164.

23. *St. Louis Post-Dispatch,* May 19, August 1, 1940.

24. Milligan, *Missouri Waltz,* 6. For the choice of Milligan see Jerome Walsh, "A Special Book Review," *Kansas City Bar Bulletin* (May 1948), 12a–d, vertical file.

25. The slogans appeared in a pamphlet, for which see "Easley, Harry—Jan.–June, 1940," box 3, Easley papers. The statement about 1908 Main Street was in Milligan's opening speech; *St. Louis Post-Dispatch,* May 19.

26. Truman to Bess W. Truman, July 24, 1939, box 10, general file, pertaining to family, business, and personal affairs; *St. Louis Post-Dispatch,* January 26, 1940; Stanley B. Pike oral history, 44–45.

27. Evans oral history, 262–65. Milligan did not believe Truman would file. When the senator asked Sermon to come to the St. Louis meeting in January 1940, he found out about it, and telephoned Sermon and asked him to come to his office. He wanted Sermon's support in the primary but said, "One Milligan [Tuck] got his tail beat by Truman and I'm not going to run if Truman files." Sermon said that if Truman did not run he would be for

Milligan. Daniels interview with Sermon, September 26, 1949, p. 22, box 1, Daniels papers.

28. *Kansas City Star*, July 21, 29; *St. Louis Post-Dispatch*, August 2.

29. *Kansas City Star*, June 21.

30. Richard S. Kirkendall, *A History of Missouri, 1919 to 1953*, 214. The position of Chambers in St. Louis politics was interesting. He had started in the 1920s as a Republican, and after the beginning of the New Deal shifted to the Democrats. Shrewd, he possessed an acute sense of how to exert power. In 1936 he ran against a white man for Democratic committeeman of the nineteenth ward but was narrowly defeated; in August 1940 he ran again and won. Taking his seat as the first black member of the Democratic city committee, he voted against Hannegan for chairman, although it was obvious that Hannegan would be elected. The chairman asked the reason for Chambers's opposition, and the black leader replied that Hannegan had not asked for his support. Mary Welek, "Jordan Chambers: Black Politician and Boss," 359.

31. For the following see Franklin D. Mitchell, *Embattled Democracy: Missouri Democratic Politics, 1919–1932*, 63–64.

32. Thomas D. Wilson, "Chester A. Franklin and Harry S. Truman: An African-American Conservative and the 'Conversion' of the Future President."

33. Ibid., 67.

34. Easley oral history, 57, 61, 64–65; Truman to Easley, August 13, 1940, "Easley, Harry—Jan.–June, 1940," box 2, Easley papers.

35. Gary Ross Mormino, *Immigrants on the Hill: Italian-Americans in St. Louis, 1882–1982*, 186. In deciding to go over to Truman in 1934, Gualdoni made a study of the then presiding judge of Jackson County: "I find he is a man of ability and high character and that he is held in the most favorable esteem with his entire section of the state where he is best known. He has lived a clean, sober and successful life. . . . Judge Truman has performed his duties with courage and ability and to the satisfaction of all the people he has represented. I find he is extremely popular both in rural sections of Jackson County, where his home is, and also in the city sections. He has served these people well and has at all times kept his word." Gualdoni papers. A highly moral man, Gualdoni insisted on principled candidates. For the 1940 primary, T. H. Van Sant to Truman, May 6, "Van Sant, T. H.," box 174, Senate–Vice President file.

36. Harper oral history, 22; Alfred Fleishman, "History and Judge Harper."

37. Interview with Mrs. Roy Harper, St. Louis, July 20, 1998.

38. Unidentified newspaper, July 6, folder 363, Clark papers.

39. *St. Louis Star Times*, July 2, "Scrapbook of clippings," box 10, Messall papers; *Kansas City Star*, August 4; Daniels interview with Henry A. Bundschu, September 28, 1949, p. 27, box 1, Daniels papers. Dickmann's papers for this period are still in the hands of his family. The mayor controlled a huge city bureaucracy and hence was very powerful.

40. Daniels interview with Truman, August 30, 1949, p. 2, box 1, Daniels papers; interview with Sermon, September 26, p. 23, ibid.

41. Harper oral history, 22–23.
42. Ibid., 14.
43. Interview with Alice Gorman, St. Louis, July 20, 1998.

Chapter 5: Aftermath
1. Evans oral history, 258.
2. Hinde oral history, 112–13.
3. There can be no question that he believed himself defeated. He wrote Dr. W. L. Brandon, "When you called me on Tuesday night, just after the Associated Press had announced my defeat, I was not in the happiest frame of mind. It is quite a stunt to be defeated and win in the same night." Letter of August 12, 1940, "Brandon letters," box 1, Daniels papers.
4. Evans oral history, 259; Steinberg, *Man from Missouri*, 176; Daniels interview with Truman, August 30, 1949, p. 6, with Mr. and Mrs. Truman, November 12, p. 55, with Margaret Truman, October 23, p. 41, box 1, Daniels papers; Margaret Truman, *Bess W. Truman*, 193.
5. Daniels interview, 41.
6. Daniels interview, September 26, 1949, 23. Mr. and Mrs. Truman dismissed as ridiculous this story of a nervously disintegrated Truman on the day after the primary, and that Mrs. Truman and Margaret cried through the night. Daniels interview, November 12, 1949, 55. Margaret believed Sermon was being spiteful, because of having run for governor in the primary of 1944 and lost—that he believed Truman had not supported him. Interview, October 23, 1949, 41. The Trumans' denial of Sermon's account of August 6–7, 1940, might seem to put his story at rest. Sermon died shortly thereafter, and did not do an oral history for the Truman Library (apart from his interview with Daniels, eventually filed with Daniels's papers); he left no papers. Sermon, however, had mentioned drinking, and the last thing Bess Truman could tolerate was serious drinking; her father and two brothers were alcoholics. It is possible that her husband might have had to make a diplomatic denial of drinking at Sermon's house.
7. An Independence lawyer and state officeholder, Thice was a Truman partisan. In 1938 when Judge Douglas was running for election to the state supreme court, Governor Stark asked Thice to write letters of support. He wrote twenty-five, to persons he knew were against Douglas, and worked for the judge's Pendergast opponent. Spencer Salisbury to Stark, August 18, 1938, folder 1034, Stark papers.

Bibliography

Manuscripts

Aylward, James P. Papers. Harry S. Truman Library, Independence, Missouri.

Barrett, James W. Papers. Western Historical Manuscript Collection, State Historical Society of Missouri, Columbia.

Barringer, Lewis T. Papers. Harry S. Truman Library.

Burrus, Rufus B. Papers. Harry S. Truman Library.

Byrnes, James F. Papers. Clemson University Library, Clemson, South Carolina.

Canfil, Fred. Papers. Harry S. Truman Library.

Clark, Bennett Champ. Papers. Western Historical Manuscript Collection, Columbia.

Cummings, Homer S. Diary. University of Virginia Library, Charlottesville.

Cuneo, Ernest. Papers. Franklin D. Roosevelt Library, Hyde Park, New York.

Daniels, Jonathan. Papers. Harry S. Truman Library.

Dickmann, Bernard F. Papers. Western Historical Manuscript Collection, Columbia.

Early, Stephen T. Papers. Franklin D. Roosevelt Library, Hyde Park, New York.

Easley, Harry. Papers. Harry S. Truman Library.

Evans, Tom L. Papers. Harry S. Truman Library.

Farley, James A. Diary. Library of Congress, Washington, D.C.

Fennelly, Joseph C. Papers. Jackson County Historical Society, Independence.

Gualdoni, Louis J. Louis C. Gualdoni, Sr., St. Louis.

Hannegan, Robert E. Papers. Harry S. Truman Library.

Hurja, Emil. Papers. Franklin D. Roosevelt Library.

Kitchen, William A. Papers. Harry S. Truman Library.

Lozier, Ralph F. Papers. Western Historical Manuscript Collection, Columbia.

Maher, Sister Patrick Ellen. Papers. Harry S. Truman Library.

Messall, Victor R. Papers. Harry S. Truman Library.

Missouri State Archives. Jefferson City, Missouri.

Mitchell, E. Y., Jr. Papers. Western Historical Manuscript Collection, Columbia.

Morgenthau, Henry, Jr. Diaries and Papers. Franklin D. Roosevelt Library.

Murphy, Frank. Papers. Bentley Library, University of Michigan, Ann Arbor.

Pendergast, Thomas J. Files. U.S. District Court, Western District, Western Division, Criminal Cases 14459, 14566, 14912, 14937, Record Group 23. National Archives and Records Administration, Central Plains Region, Kansas City.

Pendergast, Thomas J., Jr. Papers. Western Historical Manuscript Collection, Kansas City.

Reeves, Albert L. Papers. Western Historical Manuscript Collection, Kansas City.

Roosevelt, Franklin D. Papers. Franklin D. Roosevelt Library.

Snyder, John W. Papers. Harry S. Truman Library.

Stark, Lloyd C. Papers. Western Historical Manuscript Collection, Columbia.

Truman, Harry S. Papers. Harry S. Truman Library.

Vaughan, Harry H. Papers. Harry S. Truman Library.

Walsh, Jerome K. Papers. Harry S. Truman Library.

Watson, Edwin M. Papers. University of Virginia Library, Charlottesville.

Wear, Sam M. Papers. Harry S. Truman Library.
Wedow, Robert M., Sr. Collection. Western Historical Manuscript
    Collection, Kansas City.

Oral Histories

(Unless otherwise specified, all of the following oral histories are
in the Truman Library.)
Aylward, James P., by James R. Fuchs.
Barringer, Lewis T., by James R. Fuchs.
Brandt, Raymond P., by Jerry N. Hess.
Earp, John A., and Vernia Earp, by Benedict K. Zobrist.
Easley, Harry, by James R. Fuchs.
Evans, Tom L., by James R. Fuchs.
Farley, James A., by Bill Cooper. University of Kentucky Library,
    Lexington.
Farrington, Richard, by Niel M. Johnson.
Fike, Stanley R., by Jerry N. Hess.
Harper, Roy W., by James R. Fuchs.
Hinde, Edgar G., by James R. Fuchs.
Matscheck, Walter, by James R. Fuchs.
Snyder, John W., by Jerry N. Hess.
Vaughan, Harry H., by Charles T. Morrissey.

Books, Articles, Dissertations, Theses

Adler, Frank J. *Roots in a Moving Stream: The Centennial History of
    Congregation B'nai Jehudah of Kansas City, 1870–1970.* Kansas
    City: The Congregation, 1972.
Alexander, Henry M. "The City Manager Plan in Kansas City."
    Missouri Historical Review 34 (1939–1940): 145–56.
Alexander, Jack. "Missouri Dark Mule." *Saturday Evening Post* 211
    (October 8, 1938): 5–7, 32, 34, 36–39.
Anon. "The Governor of Missouri Helps Indict the Boss of Kansas
    City and Becomes a Presidential Possibility." *Life* 6, no. 17
    (April 24, 1939): 15–19.
Barker, John T. *Missouri Lawyer.* Philadelphia: Dorrance, 1949.

Beatty, Jerome. "A Political Boss Talks about His Job." *American* 115 (February 1933): 30–31, 108–9.

Bell, C. Jasper. *The Story of a Missourian*. Kansas City: Privately printed, 1971.

Brown, A[ndrew] Theodore. *The Politics of Reform: Kansas City's Municipal Government, 1925–1930*. Kansas City: Community Studies, 1958.

Brown, Andrew Theodore, and Lyle W. Dorsett. *K.C.: A History of Kansas City, Missouri*. Boulder, Colo.: Pruett, 1978.

Bundschu, Henry A. *Harry S. Truman: The Missourian*. Kansas City: *Kansas City Star*, 1949.

Burnes, Brian. "The *Kansas City Star/Times* and Its Coverage of the Civil Rights Movement through 1964." Master's thesis, University of Kansas, 1998.

Coghlan, Ralph. "Boss Pendergast: King of Kansas City, Emperor of Missouri." *Forum and Century* 97 (January–June, 1937): 67–72.

Daniels, Jonathan. *The Man of Independence*. Philadelphia: Lippincott, 1950.

Dorsett, Lyle W. *The Pendergast Machine*. New York: Oxford University Press, 1968.

———. "Truman and the Pendergast Machine." *Midcontinent American Studies Journal* 7 (1966): 16–27.

Dunar, Andrew J. *The Truman Scandals and the Politics of Morality*. Columbia: University of Missouri Press, 1984.

Dunne, Gerald T. *The Missouri Supreme Court: From Dred Scott to Nancy Cruzan*. Columbia: University of Missouri Press, 1993.

Evans, Timothy B. " 'This Certainly Is Relief!': Matthew S. Murray and Missouri: Politics during the Depression." *Missouri Historical Society Bulletin* 28 (July 1972): 219–33.

Farley, James A. *Behind the Ballots: The Personal History of a Politician*. New York: Harcourt, Brace, 1938.

———. *Jim Farley's Story: The Roosevelt Years*. New York: McGraw-Hill, 1948.

Fennelly, John Joseph. "Kansas City: 1925 to 1951." Senior thesis, Princeton University, 1952.

Ferrell, Robert H. *Harry S. Truman: A Life*. Columbia: University of Missouri Press, 1994.

———, ed. *Dear Bess: The Letters from Harry to Bess Truman: 1910–1959*. New York: Norton, 1983.

———, ed. *FDR's Quiet Confidant: The Autobiography of Frank C. Walker.* Niwot: University Press of Colorado, 1997.

Fine, Sidney. *Frank Murphy: The Washington Years.* Ann Arbor: University of Michigan Press, 1984.

Fleishman, Alfred. "History and Judge Harper." *St. Louis Business Journal* (May 27–June 2, 1991).

Garwood, Darrell. *Crossroads of America: The Story of Kansas City.* New York: Norton, 1945.

Grothaus, Larry. "Kansas City Blacks, Harry Truman and the Pendergast Machine." *Missouri Historical Review* 69 (1974): 65–82.

———. "The Negro in Missouri Politics, 1890–1941." Ph.D. diss., University of Missouri, 1970.

Hamby, Alonzo L. *Man of the People: A Life of Harry S. Truman.* New York: Oxford University Press, 1995.

Hartmann, Rudolph H. *The Kansas City Investigation: Pendergast's Downfall, 1938–1939.* Columbia: University of Missouri Press, 1999.

Haskell, Henry C., Jr., and Richard B. Fowler. *City of the Future: A Narrative History of Kansas City, 1850–1950.* Kansas City: Glenn, 1950.

Heller, Francis H. "Truman." In *The History Makers,* edited by Lord Longford and Sir John Wheeler Bennett, 32–35. New York: St. Martin's, 1973.

Helm, William P. *Harry Truman: A Political Biography.* New York: Duell, Sloan and Pearce, 1947.

Hulston, John K. *An Ozarks Lawyer's Story: 1946–1976.* Republic, Missouri: Privately printed, 1976.

Irey, Elmer L., and William J. Slocum. "How We Smashed the Pendergast Machine." *Coronet* 23 (December 1947): 67–76.

———. *The Tax Dodgers: The Inside Story of the T-Men's War with America's Political and Underworld Hoodlums.* New York: Greenberg, 1948.

Kelley, Herbert. "Youth Goes into Action." *American* 119 (February 1935): 12–13, 110–12.

Kirkendall, Richard S. *A History of Missouri, 1919 to 1953.* Columbia: University of Missouri Press, 1986.

———. "Truman and the Pendergast Machine: A Comment." *Midcontinent American Studies Journal* 7 (1966): 36–39.

Kremer, Gary R., and Antonio F. Holland, eds. *Missouri's Black Heritage*. Rev. ed. Columbia: University of Missouri Press, 1993.
———. "The Pendergast Machine and the African-American Vote." *Kawsmouth* 1 (autumn 1998): 2–12.
Larsen, Lawrence H. *Federal Justice in Western Missouri: The Judges, the Cases, the Times*. Columbia: University of Missouri Press, 1994.
———. "A Political Boss at Bay: Thomas J. Pendergast in Federal Prison, 1939–1940." *Missouri Historical Review* 86 (1991–1992): 396–417.
Larsen, Lawrence H., and Nancy J. Hulston. *Pendergast!* Columbia: University of Missouri Press, 1997.
———. "Criminal Aspects of the Pendergast Machine." *Missouri Historical Review* 91 (1996–1997): 168–80.
Lee, R. Alton. *Harry S. Truman: Where Did the Buck Stop?* New York: Lang, 1991.
McCulloch, Spencer R. " 'Boss' Pendergast Tells the Story of His Remarkable Career." *St. Louis Post-Dispatch*, September 12, 1937.
McCullough, David. *Truman*. New York: Simon and Schuster, 1992.
Maney, Patrick J. *The Roosevelt Presence: A Biography of Franklin Delano Roosevelt*. New York: Twayne, 1992.
Mason, Frank. *Truman and the Pendergasts*. Evanston, Ill.: Regency, 1963.
Mayerberg, Samuel S. *Chronicle of an American Crusader: Alumni Lectures Delivered at the Hebrew Union College, Cincinnati, Ohio, December 7–10, 1942*. New York: Bloch, 1944.
Miller, Richard Lawrence. *Truman: The Rise to Power*. New York: McGraw-Hill, 1986.
Milligan, Maurice M. *Missouri Waltz: The Inside Story of the Pendergast Machine by the Man Who Smashed It*. New York: Scribner, 1948.
Missouri, State of. *Official Manual*. Jefferson City: published biannually.
Mitchell, Ewing Y. *Kicked In and Kicked Out of the President's Little Cabinet*. Washington, D.C.: Privately printed, 1936.
Mitchell, Franklin D. *Embattled Democracy: Missouri Democratic Politics, 1919–1932*. Columbia: University of Missouri Press, 1968.
———. " 'Who Is Judge Truman?' The Truman-for-Governor Movement of 1931." *Midcontinent American Studies Journal* 7 (1966): 3–15.

Mormino, Gary Ross. *Immigrants on the Hill: Italian-Americans in St. Louis, 1882–1982*. Urbana: University of Illinois Press, 1986.

Oster, Donald B. "Reformers, Factionalists and Kansas City's 1925 City Manager Charter." *Missouri Historical Review* 72 (1977–1978): 296–327.

Otis, Merrill E. *In the Day's Work of a Federal Judge: A Miscellany of Opinions, Addresses and Extracts from Opinions and Addresses.* Kansas City: Brown-White, 1937.

Phipps, Herb. *Bill Kyne of Bay Meadows: The Man Who Brought Horse Racing Back to California.* South Brunswick, N.J.: Barnes, 1978.

Powell, Eugene James. *Tom's Boy Harry: The First Complete, Authentic Story of Harry Truman's Connection with the Pendergast Machine.* Jefferson City, Mo.: Hawthorn, 1948.

Read, Lear B. *Human Wolves: Seventeen Years of War on Crime.* Kansas City: Brown-White-Lowell, 1941.

Reddig, William M. *Tom's Town: Kansas City and the Pendergast Legend.* Philadelphia: Lippincott, 1947.

Schauffler, Edward R. "The End of Pendergast." *Forum* 102 (July 1939): 18–23.

———. *Harry Truman: Son of the Soil.* Kansas City: Privately printed, 1945.

Schmidtlein, Gene. "Harry S. Truman and the Pendergast Machine." *Midcontinent American Studies Journal* 7 (1966): 26–35.

———. "Truman the Senator." Ph.D. diss., University of Missouri, 1962.

———. "Truman's First Senatorial Election." *Missouri Historical Review* 57 (January 1963): 128–55.

Schnell, J. Christopher. "Missouri Progressives and the Nomination of F.D.R." *Missouri Historical Review* 68 (1973–1974): 269–79.

———. "New Deal Scandals: E. Y. Mitchell and F.D.R.'s Commerce Department." *Missouri Historical Review* 69 (1974–1975): 357–75.

Schnell, J. Christopher, Richard J. Collings, and David W. Dillard. "The Political Impact of the Depression on Missouri: 1929–1940." *Missouri Historical Review* 85 (1990–1991): 131–57.

Schwarz, Jordan A. *The Speculator: Bernard M. Baruch in Washington, 1917–1965.* Chapel Hill: University of North Carolina Press, 1981.

Slavens, George Everett. "Lloyd C. Stark as a Political Reformer: 1936–1941." Master's thesis, University of Missouri, 1957.

Spencer, Thomas T. "Bennett Champ Clark and the 1936 Presidential Campaign." *Missouri Historical Review* 75 (1980–1981): 197–213.

Steinberg, Alfred. *The Man from Missouri: The Life and Times of Harry S. Truman.* New York: Putnam, 1962.

Swain, Martha H. *Pat Harrison: The New Deal Years.* Jackson: University Press of Mississippi, 1978.

Truman, Harry S. *Memoirs: Year of Decisions.* Garden City, New York: Doubleday, 1955.

Truman, Margaret. *Bess W. Truman.* New York: Macmillan, 1986.

———. *Harry S. Truman.* New York: Morrow, 1973.

———. *Souvenir: Margaret Truman's Own Story.* New York: McGraw-Hill, 1956.

U.S. Senate, 77th Cong., 1st sess. *Investigation of Presidential, Vice Presidential, and Senatorial Campaign Expenditures, 1940.* Washington: Government Printing Office, 1941.

Vaughan, Harry H. "Looking Back with Gen. Harry Vaughan." *The Scroll of Phi Delta Theta* (January 1965).

Walsh, Jerome. "A Special Book Review." *Kansas City Bar Bulletin* (May 1948): 12a–d.

Welek, Mary. "Jordan Chambers: Black Politician and Boss." *Journal of Negro History* 57 (October 1972): 352–69.

Wheeler, Burton K. *Yankee from the West.* Garden City, N.Y.: Doubleday, 1962.

Where These Rocky Bluffs Meet: Including the Story of the Kansas City Ten-Year Plan, with Illustrations. Kansas City: Chamber of Commerce, 1938.

Wilson, Thomas D. "Chester A. Franklin and Harry S. Truman: An African-American Conservative and the 'Conversion' of the Future President." *Missouri Historical Review* 88 (1993–1994): 48–77.

Index